The Black Dog

REVEREND JOHN R. DOLAN

Illustrated by Paul Egel

The Black Dog
by
John R. Dolan

Illustrated by
Paul Egel

Signalman Publishing   2012
www.signalmanpublishing.com
email: info@signalmanpublishing.com
Kissimmee, Florida

Cover design by Paul Egel
Interior layout and design by Joel Ramnaraine

ISBN: 978-1-935991-58-8 (paperback)
978-1-935991-59-5 (ebook)

Library of Congress Control Number: 2012937024

SIGNALMAN
PUBLISHING

This book is dedicated to Karen Joyce Dolan, who has lived a good part of her thirty six year marriage suffering the consequences of my struggle with the Black Dog.

Karen's love, courage and human fortitude, as well as her deep faith has been a model of support.

Without Karen being there for me, the outcome of this story might be very different. I love you and thank you Karen.

John Richard Dolan

TABLE OF CONTENTS

FOREWORD

I am the master of my fate... I am the captain of my soul... —William Ernest Henley, 1875

This book describes one man's life experiences as he struggled with anxiety and depression. The book presents the mental, physical but most importantly the power of the Holy Spirit that eventually enabled John to develop resilience, and thus led him into the sunlight of a full and meaningful life.

Journey with John for almost seventy years. Travel with him from the darkest of places into the light of a full and active life; a life now for a number of years, substantially free from the presence and influence of the black dog.

Chronic anxiety and depression resulted in John seeing the world as a place where he did not feel worthy, where self-doubt and negativity consumed his creativity and his sense of humor. These were two precious characteristics that John loved in his life, and which his friends and loved ones enjoyed in return...

John, for many years, lived in a world where the positive power of the Holy Spirit seemed to be absorbed, if not lost, in a pit of negativity created by the anxiety and depression.

7

As with millions of fellow sufferers in the world, John held his suffering as his most tightly held secret. It was a secret because he regarded the condition of the "Black Dog" as a contradiction to who he felt he really was and what he was capable of contributing to the world. He felt that to reveal the secret of his anxiety and depression would be seen by the world as a sign of weakness and therefore something of which he was ashamed.

The term "Black Dog" is synonymous with the condition of anxiety and depression. It is documented that the term "Black Dog" was coined by Winston Churchill who suffered from chronic depression.

There have been other books written about experience with depression, a number of these books even use the term "Black Dog" in books' titles and references. What makes this book different is that the reader will go on this long journey together with John.

The reader will share in the actual experience of what John lived through, using the imagery of the Black Dog as a measure of his suffering, but also as a demonstration of his learning over many years how to cope with his condition.

The words "Black Dog" are intentionally written with initial capital letters to denote its strength, but it is also unreal. The capitalization is also designed to convey a sense of the Dog's persistency and the negative power that it emanated that made John's life so very difficult, and which he has fought so hard to overcome.

You may notice, however, that at the beginning and toward the very end of the book, the black dog becomes just that... no initial capitals. This is not an editorial slip; it is rather an indication that the dog had either no apparent influence or was losing its power over John's life.

With John, you will journey into the abyss. But you will then travel and experience with him, the joy as he learned techniques to overcome anxiety and depression, and how he learned to put a leash on his Black Dog. You will encounter John's growing self-awareness, but also his growing relationship with God, that ultimately prevails over the evil of the Dog.

The Black Dogs as depicted are not visions. They are imagery that represents the intensity of the attack of depression. The reader will see the Dog sometimes portrayed as a meek little puppy you want to hold in your arms and caress. At other times the Dog is seen on alert, ready to strike. But the Dog is also seen as a horrific monster, blood dripping from its fangs. This represents the ferocity of depression and anxiety and how it can attack and debilitate a sufferer.

With good reason, John saw the Black Dog as a condition that made him vulnerable to others in the world. He saw in specific people the potential of them being his enemy, ready and willing to take advantage of his situation. Also he experienced times when people did indeed take advantage of his vulnerability, adding another level of pain on top of his existing suffering. The author felt-that the Dog made him unreliable and that it produced traits of character that were better off hidden from the world.In the throes of an attack, John saw himself in a totally negative vein, without any positive attributes and he would do his utmost to ensure that other people not see him in that condition. This led to periods of total emotional and physical isolation. This, in turn, caused much pain to John's loved ones.

John, like his father before him, and millions of other people in the world, suffered in many different ways from anxiety and depression.

John has worked through the stages of learning about the disease, learning there are coping skills and providing the hope that one day he would be able to share his story with others.

The overall message and intent of this book is one of hope; it is a story of the power of sharing and love.

The book describes how staying connected to your loved ones and friends, when attacked by anxiety and depression, that the connection itself becomes the strongest defense against the Dog. The Dog can't find a way in to isolate the patient.

Combining that with a thorough understanding of the

condition through years of therapy, and securing the right balance of medication can develop a powerful resilience.

In John's story you will read how the fear and dread associated with the Black Dog has been diminished through the grace of God; fear has been replaced with the desire to teach others how the Black Dog can be restrained. How the sneaky, manipulative Dog's power is in large part removed by the sufferer simply removing the mystery of the disorder.

John has learned that once the mystery is removed, that the Black Dog condition may be shared with others in community. To enjoy the wonders of the world as the anxiety and depression dissipates, and the dog is allowed to pass by like a simple black rain cloud.

The rain cloud is replaced by the sunshine of a new day, full of hope and opportunity.

Most important of all is to allow God to enter your heart and act as the ultimate defense against the Dog.

John acknowledges the contribution made by many people in the writing of this book. The persons are named in the body of the book. Some contributors are identified by their actual names. Others prefer to use pen names. John is very grateful to all those who have helped write his story.

The book is rich in illustrations provided by the talented Paul Egel. Paul has previously worked with John in writing and publishing his first book, ***The Mushroom Farm and other reflections from a spiritual journey***.

Paul has spent many hours with John, listening to his story and then presenting images of "The Dog" and other relevant events in his story.

In 1875, the British Victorian poet, William Ernest Henley wrote the poem, *Invictus*, the Latin word meaning "unconquerable".

The author finds this poem particularly relevant to his story:

Out of the night that covers me,

Black as the pit from pole to pole,

I thank whatever God may be,

for my unconquerable soul.

In the fell clutch of circumstance,

I have not cried nor winced aloud,

Under the bludgeoning of chance,

My head is bloody but unbowed.

Beyond this place of wrath and tears

Looms but the horror of the shade,

And yet the menace of the years

Finds and shall find me unafraid.

It matters not how straight the gate,

How charged with punishments the scroll,

I am the master of my fate,

I am the captain of my soul.

—William Ernest Henley, 1875

CHAPTER 1

A Difficult Childhood

I suffered from asthma for most, if not all, of my childhood... my earliest memories include the frequent excitement and anticipation of a family outing, party or other special occasion. Resources were in short supply in post-war England and the thought of a special event made the normal excitement even more special.

However, almost inevitably, on the day of the event, I awoke with the symptoms of an incapacitating asthma attack. I have painful memories of much anticipated, happy occasions being spoiled for both me and my family by my asthma, which then became the new, unwelcome focus for the family...

Whether I wanted it or not, I felt that I became the center of the universe with this condition. I did not intentionally, or at least consciously, seek either the additional personal attention or the physical symptoms that the asthma attacks created.

There were very few medication options in the late 1940s in post-war Britain... crushed "ephedrine", a bronchodilator medicine mixed with jam on a spoon was about all that was available until I was ten years old. I remember the feeling over and over again as a child that if my whole life was going to be like this, struggling for air, day after day, that life would just not be worth it.

Then came the bronchial inhaler, and ultimately what I have always regarded as "the magic pill". Prednisone was invented in the 1950s; an anti-inflammatory medium, the drug is used to this day to treat asthma and any number of other complaints. Prednisone stopped the worst asthma attack dead in its tracks... at last it seemed I now had the opportunity to live a reasonable life.

I might stress at this point that even when beset with the worst asthma attack, I always felt loved in my family home, receiving perhaps even too much attention at times. A focus of attention, by the way, that must have been good reason to irritate any sibling, no matter how much they loved you. All these years later, I appreciate how difficult it must have been for my younger sister, Lizzie, during those times when my parents were consumed in their concern for my recovery from an asthma attack.

There is a dichotomy at this point because when I was healthy, I sometimes felt my mother did not pay enough attention to what I was telling her. I call this "the ironing board syndrome". I would sit down close to the ironing board as my mom completed her chore. I tried to choose a moment when she could not escape to other tasks and was "cornered", almost forced to listen to my issues.

I inevitably left those situations feeling empty because I was not able to convey the issue to my mom; I left with the feeling that my mom was unavailable. Perhaps what I failed to appreciate was how much work and creativity was needed to raise two children in a country blighted by post-war shortages. Also I failed to appreciate the huge amount of attention my illness demanded of my mom, and that there were other people and issues in the world other than John's asthma.

My dad also had periods of being emotionally unavailable; he would spend whole weekends "chopping firewood in the garage" or working alone in his garden, keeping out of the way. Sometimes he would suddenly be called to his office and then be working much of the weekend. I loved my dad and I know he loved me; I just did not understand his "not being there".

Every three months or so, mom and I would take the trek by train and bus to "The Great Ormond Street Hospital for Sick Children" in Central London. We went to see a certain Dr. Dunn and I can see him now, a red haired man, with a delightful manner. Unfortunately though, he had very little ammunition to work with in the form of medication or therapy to alleviate the curse of the asthma condition.

I share this detail of what is a most common disorder among children, not because of the asthma itself, but because I believe that anxiety and depression wrapped their insidious tentacles around probably each and every asthma attack.

As the first sign of asthma encroached itself into my world... it was as if I felt my personality change. I would be consumed with fear for what I was about to go through. I would withdraw into myself; social interaction, which was one of the great pleasures of my life, became unavailable to me...

My mother would know just by my physical posture as I sat in a chair in the living room... she knew what was happening to me.

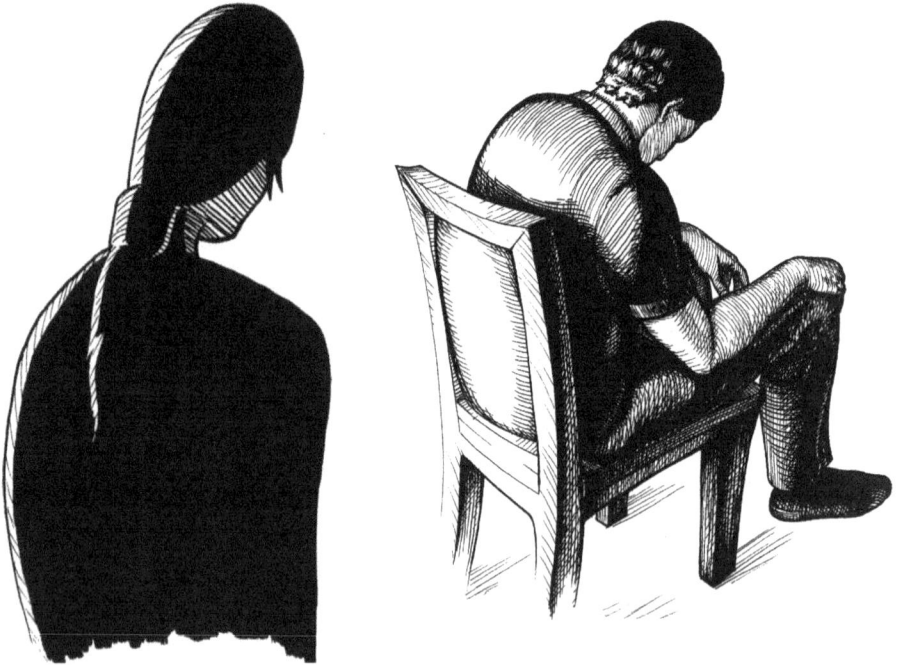

I have believed since a small child that Robert Louis Stevenson in portraying the character transformation in *The Strange case of Dr. Jekyll and Mr. Hyde* was himself familiar with the effects of depression and how it can totally change one's personality.

The other clue to depression being tied into the asthma was my feelings when the transition occurred of returning to school from a period of absence due to illness.

We all have "normal" levels of apprehension and worry, particularly when one, as a child, missed vital lessons or instruction. Particularly so in a highly competitive environment such as the school I attended. But when my dad, who invariably gave me a ride to school when I had been absent, asked me how I was feeling, I remember physically shaking. Fear wracked my body and mind; I would mentally berate myself, "this weakling, this softie, how was he going to climb back and restore his credibility as one of the leaders of his class".

With the advantage of hindsight and experience, all the signposts indicated anxiety and depression; conditions that were to accompany me, probably for a lifetime.

I remember my friend Andrew as being particularly sensitive to my tendency to anxiety and my obsession with transitions. Whenever he saw me suffering in this way, Andrew would just say to me, "Keep a cool head." Thinking back, I am sure he has never realized how helpful and meaningful this was for me.

Another school friend was Robert McDermott. "Mac", the friendly giant, as I have always known him, has always been physically and spiritually the best example of a human being that I have had the pleasure to call a friend.

I remember one particular occasion; I was on the bus on the way to school and I felt a growing anxiety... knowing full well that I was about to experience an asthma attack. Two things then occurred: the attack occurred and I felt near physical collapse. But almost at the same moment my friend Mac boarded the bus.

Mac came over to me and from my facial expression and physical posture he knew immediately what was going on. He said, "Just lean on me; no one will know!"

I leaned on my friend Mac many times growing up. He knew the combination existed. He knew that I was having to battle two or even three demons; asthma, anxiety and depression, pride and embarrassment... all wrapped up together in a package that at times made me wonder if I would survive.

Thinking back, I am sure the black dog was lying in the weeds waiting for his opportunity to strike; but he would have to wait a while.

My life at home, like any other family, was at times tense; whether it be attributed to my health issues, or just four strong-minded individuals who loved each other unconditionally, but nonetheless held strong opinions, opinions on everything from religion to table manners.

The effect from combining some, or all of these ingredients was on occasion, as with any other families, disputes or rows. The after effects of these rows never lingered, but nonetheless at the time they occurred there was "fire and brimstone".

These family ructions would leave me physically shaking, but the love in our family was strong enough to withstand a door that was slammed one day, so hard, that I thought our brick house would fall down. There were never any repercussions; our love for each other was much too strong for that to happen.

As a footnote here. In view of the "lively" verbal exchanges in our home, it was rather strange that our paternal grandmother always claimed that we definitely had no Irish blood in our veins. This, on top of our having a name like Dolan. Not many Dolans in Wales for sure, but in Dublin, Ireland, one inch thickness in the telephone directory was given over to the name Dolan.

Also my grandmother never admitted that my granddad was, in fact, an Irish immigrant from County Cork.

CHAPTER 2

Game Playing

As a child, the doctor used to say to me, "Don't worry, John, you will grow out of this asthma thing." That was most reassuring at the time; the only problem was he failed to attach any dates to the prediction.

Some fifteen years later, when I moved from Wales to London in 1965, the doctor's prediction came to fruition. I was twenty three years of age, and the asthma had not only subsided, it had disappeared from my life. I had left my parents' home for the first time, I had to manage my own affairs and I was determined to succeed.

The black dog was presumably still lying somewhere in the weeds, but he was invisible to me in my life and played no part in my life for decades to come.

How was it that the dog lay dormant for all those years? The only answer I am able to provide is there was just no room for the dog in my life at that point.

Looking back, a number of major changes had occurred in my life, all of them fully occupying both my mind and my emotions.

Firstly I was pursuing a career as a CPA (British Chartered Accountant). This was an enormous test of my intelligence, my perseverance and my social flexibility.

Secondly, I was immersed in the sport of rowing. I was part of a squad of eight young men rowing for Vesta Rowing Club in London.

As a squad, we trained together, all seasons for two years, six days a week. We competed at every "regatta", i.e. competitive rowing events, that it was possible to schedule. We loved our sport and our time together and in due course won more than our share of events.

This bonding with the rowing squad, my competitive nature and my position at "number four", the engine room of the racing shell, made me feel I was a vital part of the organization.

I felt respected, and I was extremely physically fit for the first time in my life.

The social life attached to the rowing is a book in itself, but not one that I can write about, particularly as a responsible parent, grandparent and minister of the church. But let us just say I had a wonderful time.

Thirdly during those years I worked for one of the top public accounting firms and I secured my degree and my CPA (Chartered Accountant's) practicing certificate.

I was confident in myself and in my abilities at multiple levels. There was no room for doubt or fear. There was only room for optimism, and in search of wider horizons I decided to apply for a twelve month contract to work in the United States, in Chicago, Illinois. This was in August 1969.

The period of my teens and early twenties had undoubtedly been one of the best times in my life. I had performed well academically; I was a winner in the rowing world and I was managing my own life independent from my family of origin. I was also entirely free from both asthma and depression.

On November 3rd, 1970, I arrived at O'Hare Airport in Chicago.

I felt on top of the world, both mentally and physically. I was excited about this adventure of working and living in America. I felt well prepared, but what I didn't notice was that in my baggage deep in the hold of the Pan Am Boeing 747 was a quiet, well be-haved, and inor-dinately patient black dog.

The black dog who, other than for a couple of brief appear-ances, would lie dormant in my life for a further fourteen years.

But this was a Dog that had the potential to destroy my life; in fact my Black Dog did his very best to destroy my business and pro-fessional life over a period of more than twenty years.

CHAPTER 3

Vulnerability

In 1972, my work took me to manage a series of hospital financial audits in a number of southern States. I felt a great sense of personal freedom and responsibility: demands were placed on me for a high level of professionalism in my work, and I lived with the support of a generous expense account. This was an exciting and satisfying time in my life.

One of the States that I worked in was Florida, and this required setting up an administrative office in St. Petersburg. My secretary in this office, "Sheila", announced to us all one day at the office that she had separated from her husband. What followed was some bizarre behavior; and Sheila, although some thirty years my senior, nonetheless seemed to look to me as her father figure, which was flattering, but secretly alarming.

My emotional response was a growing fear and dread of what might happen as a result of her behavior. Would she harm herself and in some way involve me in the event? Was she suffering from a mental disorder; what was my responsibility in such a circumstance?

One would expect a level of apprehension in such circumstances, but for me my anxiety grew out of all reasonable proportions, at least based on my experience of "normal" feelings. Very quickly my fear of this situation grew to the point of my not being able to leave my apartment, let alone go to the office.

The Black Dog at last had found the opportunity to make my life difficult and was snarling around me for more than two weeks. My life was full of fear and dread and the trigger clearly had been the abnormal behavior of my secretary.

The dreadful feelings, of extreme anxiety and depression, were eerily familiar to me; I had experienced them before, but not for a long, long time.

A trip back to Chicago, then meetings and social events with my colleagues and friends managed to contain the Dog. None of my colleagues had the faintest idea of what I had experienced in Florida. I made certain they did not know about what I considered to be, an unacceptable weakness in my character.

Scroll forward about five years; two years after our

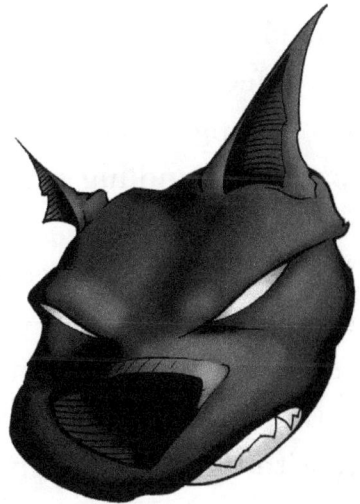

marriage and my wife Karen had just given birth to our daughter, Michelle Elizabeth. It was one of the happiest moments of our lives, and from the moment of her birth, Michelle conveyed a sense of purpose and urgency.

At Michelle's wedding in 2003, I made the comment that at the moment she was born, Michelle looked at her dad as if to say, come on none of this sentimental stuff, I have things to do and places to go.

A few hours after her birth, I was walking alone down Michigan Avenue in Chicago and I pondered the dramatic change that Michelle's birth would bring to our lives. A feeling of joy filled my heart; but there was another feeling, a feeling of anxiety as to whether I was capable of handling the responsibility of this newborn child.

I am told this is a frequent reflection, particularly for a first time parent, but with me I wondered whether the intensity of the fear and anxiety was normal. I believe the Black Dog showed his fearsome, ugly, face to interfere with the joy of that moment.The feelings of fear and dread stayed with me until Michelle and Karen were safely home with me in our apartment, about a week later.

In early 1979, Karen and I had been married almost four years. One morning, as I sat on the train headed downtown from our home in Western Springs, I was thinking about a relatively routine issue that I had to deal with that day. It was the type of issue that I had dealt with literally hundreds of times; normally it would be as taxing as "a walk in the park".

Suddenly I felt overwhelmed with fear and dread. The feeling was inexplicable to me, but I felt so consumed by the negative emotion that when I arrived at Union Station in Chicago, I caught the next train home.

The journey home was horrendous, and I sank lower and lower the closer we got to my destination. My mind was crammed full of negatives: *I am losing it; what a personal weakness, I am a failure; what a lack of character and moral fiber; how would I explain this to my dear wife?*

The Dog had made a savage and unexpected appearance, but at that stage in my life I had no idea what was happening. Within twenty-four hours I had seen

my doctor, the condition was diagnosed as stress-related and within two or three days I was back to feeling "normal".

In 1980, I was selected by senior management at Blue Cross and Blue Shield of Chicago, as one of only four managers, for an advanced management development program. The president of the company sent me a handwritten, highly complementary note. He also invited the four of us to attend an upcoming senior managers' retreat.

At the retreat, I generally felt comfortable and positive about things. I received a number of compliments from people whom I respected and admired.

On the second morning, I was walking alone down a hallway and I saw the company president approaching me, and he was smiling broadly.

My reaction to this friendly, welcoming approach was as if I had been hit with a stun gun; I was overwhelmed with negative thoughts, *If you talk to him he will soon see you as the fraud you really are; I am sure he will tell you that he has changed his mind and I am off the program; how are you going to explain your presence here, you are a presumptive fool.*

In an instant, the Black Dog consumed all my confidence and positive feelings, so much so that I could not face the down to earth, delightful gentleman who was the president of our company.

Instead I hustled off in the opposite direction, rather like a scalded cat.

At what should have been a moment of personal reinforcement, the Dog savaged me viciously and I will always believe that this damaged my personal confidence, and in turn probably my career at Blue Cross.

I have never felt so weak and pathetic; so embarrassed by my own actions. I had let down all those that believed in me. I felt so bad that I packed my suitcase and left that place, using what would become the familiar excuse of "not feeling well".

About six months later, I was in my office at Blue Cross, reviewing some material that I had just distributed to another division in the company. I discovered an error in the numbers. In the scheme of things it was not material and the error certainly didn't change the conclusion of the particular analysis.

I was pleased with the work I had done on this analysis; it was creative and well prepared. But in the space of five seconds, the error consumed me. I was filled with fear and dread and I remember actually physically trembling. The Black Dog had snuck in and was ecstatic in being able to exploit my vulnerability.

I remember thinking, *my boss will fire me immediately, I will be embarrassed in front of the other division and my workmates. How can I escape from this situation? There you go; you don't even have the guts to face up to things, you are an absolute loser.*

I remember leaving a note for my boss and going home "sick". The Dog was showing his power and I still had no understanding of what was going on.

As I travelled home on the train, I began to be consumed with fear for the next time the Black Dog would make one of his "cameo appearances". How can I handle all my responsibilities with this anxiety and depression hanging over me?

I thought about why was I unable to engage in any discussion with my friends, extended family, clergy or doctor about why these terrible "attacks" of anxiety and depression were occurring?

The condition was a secret that I intended to keep to myself and my immediate family, and it would remain so.

I was fearful that the attacks were probably getting worse, but I decided I would continue to cover up the situation with my well-used plethora of lies and fabrications, the most common being sudden, unexplained illnesses.

CHAPTER 4

The Dog Bares His Teeth

In 1983, after thirteen successful years at Chicago Blue Cross, I went to work for a prominent teaching hospital in Chicago. I had been approached by the chief financial officer of the hospital to be the controller of the hospital's for-profit venture services company.

I left on good terms with Frank, my boss, and all my associates at the Blues, but very soon after joining my new employer, I felt the presence of the Black Dog. Perhaps this was triggered by my leaving a workplace where I was well known and respected, to face the relative unknown.

In my new job I was to report to "Janet", an excellent professional, someone who I really liked and whom I felt comfortable working with.

In the context of the Black Dog showing me its ugly head, I will never forget Janet, talking with my wife Karen, at a hospital social event...

Janet said, "It was as if John, on occasion, was transformed into a different person. One day John was in a meeting with me and was his normal self; humorous, focused, energetic and knowledgeable. Then in a matter of minutes he would be nervous, withdrawn, distracted and even his skin took on a different, grayish, pallor."

Thus chronic depression, "The Black Dog" started to make his hellish presence more frequent and the beginning of an increasingly unwelcome and seemingly uncontrollable presence in my life.

I would always have a plausible reason for my condition, whatever that "condition" was. Whether it be my wife and young family, my boss or friends, it made no difference. But I was now employed by one of the most prestigious medical groups in the country. I was the Central Hospital Medical Group's financial controller, and the Dean kept his eye on me. As he said at the time they "relied on me too much for me to fall by the wayside".

One day I was in the midst of an "attack", the term I have always used for the onset of a bout of severe depression, but this time the symptoms appeared during an executive board meeting. The Dean approached me after the meeting. "John, call your wife and have her bring in the necessaries, you are being admitted to the cardiac department for diagnostic tests." I had no way out of this, and perhaps there was some physical reason for these attacks, and a physical condition would be much more acceptable to me than a mental health problem.

In late 1984, two days and a $10,000 hospital bill later, I was given the "all clear". The diagnosis, "John is under a little stress and needs to play more racquetball."

The Black Dog raised himself up, just grinned at me and then disappeared from sight. My life went on as before, or did it?

In 1986, I was approached by the medical staff at another teaching hospital in Chicago, at that time still an active, 400+ bed teaching hospital with approximately 700 affiliated physicians. They hired me to create an all-staff medical group organized to contract with HMOs and other managed care organizations.

The first three years as CEO of the South-

side Hospital Doctors' Group was a huge professional success. The group grew very quickly and within the three years became the third largest medical group of its kind in Chicago. I became well known and highly respected in Chicago and the Midwest.

The member doctors saw a rapid growth in their patient volume and so everyone treated me as if I were the "second coming". But the underlying financial weakness of the hospital was like a millstone around the group's neck and gradually the financial status of the doctors group started to deteriorate.

The Black Dog had lain dormant for three years as a result of my personal success in my job. But now the Dog reappeared; he appeared well behaved, did not display much emotion, merely wanting me to know he was again present in my life. The Dog, of course, chose to reappear in my life, just as the worry and stress resulting from my new responsibilities began to build.

The job proved to be an even more stressful job than at my former job. The hospital was financially on an accelerating downward spiral that not even the most creative managers could reverse. In fact the hospital no longer exists, having filed for bankruptcy protection in 2008, and in 2010 the buildings were demolished.

In the late 1980s the Black Dog was almost a constant source of complication and suffering in my life. Nothing could shake its presence, and the Dog brought with it the most terrible fear and dread, it even took away my sense of humor. My humor has always been something that I have enjoyed a great deal; it was one of my personal traits that helped me keep a sometimes complex world in perspective.

The Black Dog also stifled my creativity, it replaced optimism with doubts. It made it intolerable for me to be in the public eye because I felt that everyone would know I was a fraud and did not deserve the income and status I was blessed with at that time.

The Black Dog created a disconnect from reality; from family, from friends and other loved ones. The Dog created a disconnect from the excitement and challenges of the job; it separated me from my colleagues. The Black Dog also created a damaging disconnect in my spiritual life...

William Holman Hunt's famous painting "The Light of the World", shows Christ knocking at humanity's door, but the door handle is on the inside of the door, meaning only we can open the door to let Him in to our lives. As human beings we have the means to connect or disconnect our relationship with God.

The Black Dog made it very difficult for me to live in

any true sense of the word. The Dog made it particularly difficult for me in my relationship with God because the Black Dog paralyzed me and made me unable to turn the handle and open the door.

I have described one impact of the anxiety and depression as distorting my physical view of the world. It was like looking at the world through an uneven, misshapen lens. It is as if I looked at life through an aquarium. The objects on the other side of an aquarium are distorted by the effect of the glass and the water.

The objects are no different than the rest of the world sees them; but for me, suffering from anxiety and depression, the objects appeared twisted, deformed, and unreal.

That is exactly the way the world looks when the Black Dog has you in his wretched grasp.

The following story is one of the many examples that would have haunted me for the rest of my life if it wasn't for the Grace of God and the love and strength of faith in our Lord Jesus Christ.

It is a story of a career responsibility that normally would have been a routine assignment for me. But I was beset by the Black Dog and my view of the world had become distorted and the task turned into a monster.

It was 1986 and I was scheduled to be the featured speaker at a physicians' symposium at a well known hotel on the north side of Chicago. More than 200 physicians had already responded that they would attend. I was well prepared and was at my attorney's office putting the final pieces together for the presentation.

The Dog descended on me as if out of nowhere. One minute I was a proficient professional, the next minute I felt as if I was a fraud on my way to the gallows.

I made an excuse to leave my attorney's office and, since I had a couple of hours before the time for the presentation, I called my wife, Karen to pick me up. I could not locate her... and by now I was physically shaking.... so I called my thirteen year old daughter, Michelle, who happened to be home that day. Michelle, in her usual calm, skillful way calmed me, and said she would contact Mom and they would pick me up at a certain spot.

Karen and Michelle got me home, but I felt so full of fear that I ended up curled up into a fetal position under my desk in my office at home, trembling and unable to speak coherently.

Karen and Michelle literally talked me out of the attack. Without the advantage of medication at that point, this was no mean achievement. The fact that I trusted them both implicitly was the magic formula. They both treated the event as if it was commonplace and I slowly came back to normal.

Karen drove me to the symposium; I gave my presentation and received many compliments. No-one had the slightest clue as to the suffering I had experienced that afternoon, and which Karen and Michelle had witnessed.

The effect of this on me, however, was not to be proud of my recovery or thankful for Michelle and Karen for their being there for me. The resulting effect was to unnerve me more and more, and I at last acceded to the idea that I needed professional help.

In the face of my Black Dog, my professional life was sliding downhill at an ever-quickening pace. As if out of nowhere, the Black Dog would grab me by the throat, and my life was in danger of turning into an emotional and spiritual bloodbath.

But the rest of the world, other than my immediate family, was oblivious to what was happening to me. Skills developed over many years helped me build a very effective wall of denial.

I would not allow the world to see me as I saw myself in that state of depression. I regarded myself as a weak, cowardly, fearful wretch, because I could not just "snap out of it and count my blessings".

CHAPTER 5

Suffering

The suffering caused by the Black Dog became a heavy burden to bear in my life. To be a good husband, a loving and active father; to be the head of a 300 physician corporation was all hard enough at 42 years old... but the Black Dog's incessant violent intrusions into my life would have become too much to bear if it wasn't for my deep faith in Jesus Christ.

This faith was tested countless times, but any disconnection from my faith caused by the Dog was only temporary. Gradually, albeit slowly, over a period of many years, I realized Jesus was always with me, even in the darkest moments. I knew He was there with me even when I felt worthless, even when I felt unreliable and unable to meet my responsibilities to the world around me.

The Dog would make me question how a highly educated, experienced individual could be at the same time a fraud, a coward, who couldn't face what was expected of him. The tapes of my grandmother's voice would play in my head, *Buck up, John, what on earth do you have to be depressed about? There are a lot of other people worse off than you and they get up every day and face the world, why should you be any different?*

All very true, but it was as if I always knew that the attacks of depression were not logical, or based on problems real or imaginary. It was as if my persona changed; and I did not like the transformation.

One of the worst features of the battle with the Black Dog were the lies and pretences, and acting out I went through, to keep the Black Dog as my secret; my dreadful shameful secret. The secret that the outgoing, creative John was in fact a weak, shame-ridden, distorted individual who was of no value to neither man nor beast.

As I have already indicated, my immediate loved ones, Karen my wife now for more than thirty six years, my thirty four year old daughter Michelle and my thirty two year old son, David, have always been aware of their husband and dad's struggles with the Black Dog. It was never a secret to my immediate family and in all our years together I have never experienced a single moment of meanness from my family relating to my Black Dog when considering how much it must have disturbed their lives.

There was, however, an underlying irritation and even anger in my family resulting from a growing number of occasions when, suddenly, out of the blue, I would not be emotionally available to them.

The pressures of my job grew immensely. One day the light went on for me; I realized that the negative forces at work in that setting; a deterioration in the payer mix of the community the hospital served was having a far greater detriment on the future of our business than the best administrative and medical management in the world. But I was stubborn, and proud, and I would not admit defeat. And the Dog loved every minute of it.

I became very depressed, to the point of seriously wondering whether life was worth the suffering. All I had to do was to drive at full speed into the guard rail on the highway overpass.

I believe that it was only my strong faith and the love exhibited by my immediate family, which enabled me to tolerate the fear and dread and the bad feelings about myself that hung like a dirty black pall over my life.

Then a new complication; the Board of Directors at the medical group decided they could no longer tolerate my mysterious illnesses and continuing absences from my job. My time of using sometimes elaborate excuses to hide the Black Dog had run out.

The Black Dog was ecstatic: *I have this Dolan guy on the run. Now I will make him really suffer.* Sure enough the condition became worse than ever. When I was at home hiding behind my "defenses", the temporary relief from the pressures of the job had little or no positive impact on the pain and suffering that still struck me down without any notice... I was beginning to understand what hell is all about.

One day I was sitting in my large office along with large bronze plaques on my desk, "John R. Dolan, Chief Executive Officer". I would receive calls from the heads of various organizations around the city. Accomplished people would visit my office to ask my opinion about complex issues.

One of the most well known and successful healthcare consultants in modern day Chicago visited my office in 1993 to seek my advice whether he should start a healthcare consulting business. In the real world I was indeed, well regarded, but The Black Dog would interpret this as "I was a big shot, full of my own importance"...

I was highly respected in my chosen profession, but however many times I told myself this, I could not believe it.

The very next day after the visit from the healthcare consultant, I was asked to resign by the Medical Group Board of Directors.

I would like to add a couple of observations on the Board's action. The Black Dog had a strong ally on the Board of Directors. The Medical Director, who we will call Patrick, always appeared envious of my business skills. I was always aware that Patrick plunged a figurative knife into my back at the very moment when I needed compassion and help the most.

Black Dogs must love the "Patricks" of this world.

My attacks of depression had become more acute, more frequent, and more debilitating for longer periods of time. The ability to hide the impact of the savagery of the Black Dog gradually evaporated, and I suffered the consequence, I lost my job.

It also may be of interest to note that the fact that I worked within the medical community made no difference to my being let go. In fact, the disdain and intolerance that many medical doctors appeared to hold for mental illness in those days may have made it more difficult for me in that setting.

Later in the same week that I was let go, I was standing in our kitchen at home; I was alone other than an abundance of negative thoughts. The feelings were manifested in the gruesome, ugly face of my imaginary Black Dog, looking immensely satisfied with himself. I remember some of the negative thoughts as if coming from the Dog's foul mouth, *Now who has the upper hand, If I were you John I would just end it all.*

The Dog continued, *you are an embarrassment to anybody or anyone that had faith in you. This is about what you are worth; penniless, without a job, no prospects and your large fancy office is now the spare bedroom.*

The smile on the Dog's face was almost vengeful, *you ain't seen nothing yet, now I will make you really suffer.*

I was approaching the bottom of the emotional pit of depression. But at this moment God reached out to me. A priest friend handed me two lifelines, neither of which impressed me at the time, but which I later came to appreciate would help to radically change my life.

The first was a question posed by a friend who was an Episcopal priest... "John, have you ever considered becoming an ordained deacon in the Church?" The question seemed absurd, why on earth would someone ask me this question at probably the lowest point in my life?

The second lifeline was a name, the name of a psychologist, who we will call "Bob", whose clients included two of the most well known Chicago professional sports teams. My friend said to me, "I have a sense that you are going through a rough time, if anyone can help you, I believe Bob can be a great support." The idea of my needing that kind of help seemed equally absurd!

I put both these thoughts and opportunities safely into my back pocket and somehow, life went on.

CHAPTER 6

New Ventures or Mere Distractions?

From the moment my priest friend posed the question to me whether I had ever considered becoming an ordained deacon in our Episcopal church, I gave it serious consideration.

I prayerfully considered whether God was calling me to change my life. All this depression and pain wrapped around my life and career, what was it telling me? Was there a reason, a purpose for it all?

In late 1991, I entered a process of discernment that would eventually lead me to Deacon School (Seminary) in 1993, followed by ordination in 1996.

I loved the academic program; I excelled in the writing and preaching elements, and I don't think I missed one class or retreat in three years because of anxiety or depression.

The Black Dog, during this time, stood and silently observed me, showing little or no interest in my pursuits, but neither was the Dog interfering. It was as if this stage of my life and this particular track I was on, made me less vulnerable to depression.

The rest of my life was still vulnerable to anxiety and depression but I gradually began to learn on my own more about the condition. I learned that it probably had a hereditary component and in "very lay terms", that the primary cause was probably due to a chemical imbalance in the brain. That the normal "balancers" in the brain such as endorphins were probably not being generated or working properly.

However, no matter the level of intellectual understanding of depression I had acquired, it made no difference to how I felt when the attacks came on.

I would still isolate myself from the world as best I could. I would unplug the telephone; reschedule any meetings usually with feeble excuses. I would postpone any family, friends or other commitments I had previously committed to when I was healthy.

When attacked by the Black Dog, my whole view of myself, my abilities, my morals and knowledge of the

world would be negative. I could see no value in my being alive and how could God love such a useless individual with no value to man or beast.

The feelings were all wretched, even writing about them and reliving them makes me feel bad.

I would misconstrue everything that was said to me. No creative thoughts. No safe places except with my wife Karen and the kids, but I am told by one member of the family that I did a good job in shielding our daughter Michelle and our son David from how I felt about myself during those episodes.

In the worst throes of an attack just getting out of bed in the morning was a major accomplishment. But it was the sense of self-loathing that was the hardest symptom to deal with ...and the disconnection from friends and family and spiritual disconnection.

But now I did have a spiritual director associated with my deacon training and I always had my Karen, how she must have suffered, and how frustrating to see the man she chose to marry, from Karen's perspective at least, the talented, energetic, focused professional become a mere shadow of himself when in the midst of an attack.

The Black Dog relished these attacks; it was as if his fangs would plunge deep into my heart and try to destroy my very existence.

But I had the most powerful ally, the connection I had built in my relationship with Jesus Christ.

When faced with the power of faith exhibited particularly through prayer, it was as if the Dog would became dumbfounded, confused, not knowing what to do next.

The Dog, probably for the first time, was on the defensive. The Black Dog, however powerful, was no match for the power of the Holy Spirit.

In my discernment process for the diaconate, I was afraid that my struggle with the Black Dog would be seen as a negative. That this might be considered a form of mental instability and thus preclude my participation in this branch of ordained ministry.

Nothing could have been further from the truth. I was told if anything, my battle with the Black Dog would qualify me as being able to be more compassionate with the millions of people who suffer from this disease.

My cache of support mechanisms was growing by the day... and the Dog was not at all pleased. But I was also to discover that the Dog had not even hinted at the degree of suffering he was capable of inflicting on me.

I was experiencing some major changes and conflicts in my life. The Black Dog's power and negative influence on me was continuing to grow; at the same time the road to ordained ministry was a road full of positive learning, full of faith and prayer.

Two opposing forces were at play in my life but it was not clear which one would prevail. The Dog was a formidable foe and was intent on savaging me to a much greater degree, given the slightest opportunity.

CHAPTER 7

Change in Direction

Removing the stress of managing the medical group had little or no impact on the depression. If anything it made it worse and my slide into the pit continued, unabated.

Many sufferers from anxiety and depression tell the same story; that the very worst feature of the disease is waking up in the morning and the experience of an attack in progress. I will describe the experience.

The first feeling is wishing you could stay asleep forever—that life itself was an impossible challenge. The second feeling is to pull the bedcovers over your head and pray or call on someone or some entity to provide relief.

Then the specifics kick in; each issue you are dealing with in your life turns profoundly negative, if not insurmountable. In other words one loses perspective on issues that all of us as human beings have to face and deal with on a daily basis...

Then the shame and the familiar tapes kick in. Get up, be a man, face up to your challenges... what's the worst that can happen to you?

Well, for sufferers in the abyss caused by depression, the worst that can happen is that you jump off a bridge, or stand in front of a fast moving train or automobile, or slam your car into the median on the highway.

Dreadful, inward looking, self absorbed thoughts; all, of course, focused on somehow obtaining relief from the suffering. In that situation there was no room or ability to consider the impact of your potential actions on your nearest and dearest.

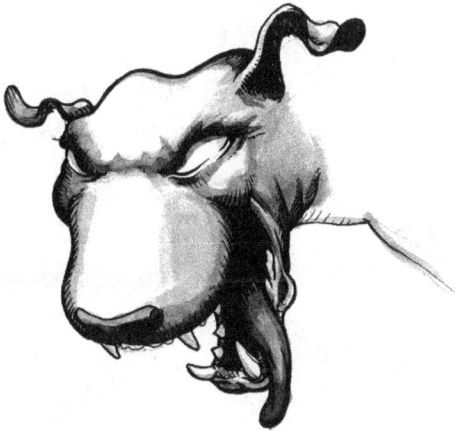

The Black Dog, grinning from ear to ear, salivated and growled as I endured the pain of waking up in the morning.

The subsequent feeling was pain from my isolation and the resulting loneliness; the shame that I felt, because I could not deal with the most routine tasks and responsibilities. Molehills became mountains to climb; pulling back the bedcovers and going through the routines of showering and shaving in the morning became insurmountable tasks in themselves.

The pain caused by disconnection from many of my

most enjoyable personal skills and feelings. The pain resulting from the spiritual disconnect. The pain of failing to meet my responsibilities as a father, a husband, a professional and an important lay member of our church community. The pain of knowing that I am a fraud, devoid of talent, devoid of a single feature that could be of value to humanity.

So many people, who suffer the rigors of anxiety and depression, have told me they understand, and live with, these feelings, and they remain the most closely guarded, personal secrets. Depression is very thorough in its destructive power, and the insistence on total and complete secrecy is one of its worst features.

If the telephone rang, I would have my wife Karen answer it if she was home. If she was not home, I would unplug the phone, close the drapes and live in complete isolation. No-one except my wife Karen and our young children, Michelle and David, were allowed inside the perimeter that was my "protection" from the Black Dog.

The very same lines of defense designed to protect myself also acted as an obstruction for contact with people and situations I most enjoyed. When an attack was at its worst, I could not even communicate with my two closest friends, Frank or Nigel.

The Dog was not hindered in any way by my "defenses"; in fact, from the Dog's perspective, he was delighted at the mental prison I created. The Dog's constant presence, prowling around the defenses, just added to the realization that I had no way of escaping the dark feelings, the feeling as if one is about to slide into a black hole.

In order to maintain my sanity, my distorted reasoning determined that I had to find some ways to escape these moments in my life. I convinced myself that I needed to have some relief from the times when the Black Dog attacked me and created for me a world full of fear and dread.

When I was a child struggling with asthma and depression, I built my "house at the end of the yard". The house was made of random pieces of wood and fabric. I found a fabric cover from an old motorcycle which was a perfect roof. But the whole structure was designed so that I had somewhere to go that was mine, and when I felt bad, I could escape from the world.

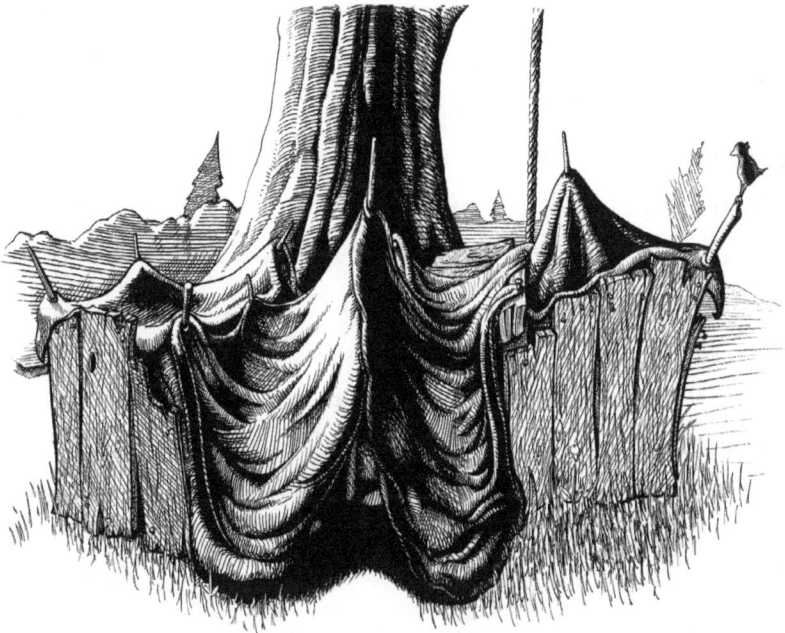

The structure grew over a period of years. It was constructed around the base of a tree and eventually the ramshackle structure became quite well known in the neighborhood.

"My house at the end of the yard" was an escape mechanism, a bolt hole for the times when it was just too difficult for me, even as a child, to deal with the issues of the world.

My family of origin, my mom, dad and my sister, Lizzie, were all very respectful of those times when I would seek refuge in "my house at the end of the yard".

I will never forget a time, however, when a friend of my mother was visiting and asked my mom where I was. Well, I was in my "house" at the end of the yard, but rather than respecting my privacy, my mom's friend walks to the end of the yard and starts shouting to me "why are you skulking in that pile of junk". She then started to pull off the cover which acted as my roof.

I was so upset that I was trembling. But I had a strong ally which was my mom, and she soon put an end to her friend's insensitivity.

Some thirty plus years later, in the 1980s, I remember, at a time when the Black Dog was close to winning the battle for my life, I considered the various methods of escape, let us call them impulsive, some might say self-indulgent excesses, available to me. The excesses incidentally did not include building another house at the end of our yard; one house was quite enough even to house my Black Dog!

The excesses, in due course, all caused their own problems for me and my family's lives. The excesses were exciting, they were my secret, and I felt not even the Black Dog knew about them. I was later to learn that this acting out was most destructive and the Black Dog was right in the middle, helping me plan these activities.

I learned that while I thought the activities were merely a way for me to gain some temporary pleasure or relief from the depression, that, in fact, it was a symptom of how much control the Dog had established on my normal life, and behavior.

The excesses were the process of acting out against self-imposed defenses against an attack of depression. The excesses included over-eating, self-medication through the use of alcohol, unacceptable moral behavior and unplanned, spur of the moment trips to far reaching places without regard to family budget, commitments and responsibilities at home.

The escape routes also included vague thoughts of possible suicide, but thank God, my faith always excluded that as an option.

My excessive use of alcohol occurred frequently during family get-togethers. When I consumed too much, my target invariably was my daughter, Michelle. The kind, loving dad turned into a mean, aggressive person who my daughter disliked intensely. This led to tension at the time and which has carried over to these days when Michelle is a mother herself and who loves her dad but who is also sensitive to her dad's consumption of alcohol at family events.

The Black Dog just stood and watched when I ventured down one or more of these exciting, scary roads, without regard to my loved ones, my reputation, my responsibilities and other positive characteristics that are part of my "normal" persona.

The Black Dog continued to wallow in his success, but the Dog did not have to do very much, John's own self-destructive behavior was doing his work for him.

The Black Dog dominated my personal landscape about one week in a month, thus I was not totally disabled. I believe the professional term is that I would be regarded as a "high functioning depressive".

I was able to work in my profession and during these years was still able to do some creative work.

In early 1990, after "leaving" the medical group, a number of my former colleagues in the healthcare industry contacted me and encouraged me to build my fledgling healthcare consulting practice. I was an expert in finance and I was one of the few professionals who had worked for both the payers and the provider community; thus I was ideally positioned to be in demand.

That is exactly what happened. The ground floor fourth bedroom in our home, to this very day, has served me admirably as my office.

I soon garnered a number of clients; my former secretary from the medical group joined me. My firm began its business that was to continue for more than twenty years.

In later years, I was told that during the discussions about my leaving the medical group there was some discussion about my plans to create a consulting business. Someone made what they considered to be the very humorous comment, which caused considerable laughter in the room.

Maybe John Dolan's miniscule consulting business would last longer than the great hospital institution itself.

What an absurd thought at the time, but, in fact, that is exactly what happened.

The Black Dog was not at all pleased with my initial success, and his expression showed great displeasure. Now having my own consulting firm I could more readily establish my own schedule. I still had pressure from work obligations, but it was different and more manageable. Was the pendulum starting to swing in John's favor?

I also started thinking about the referral that I had been given... to the counselor, "Bob".

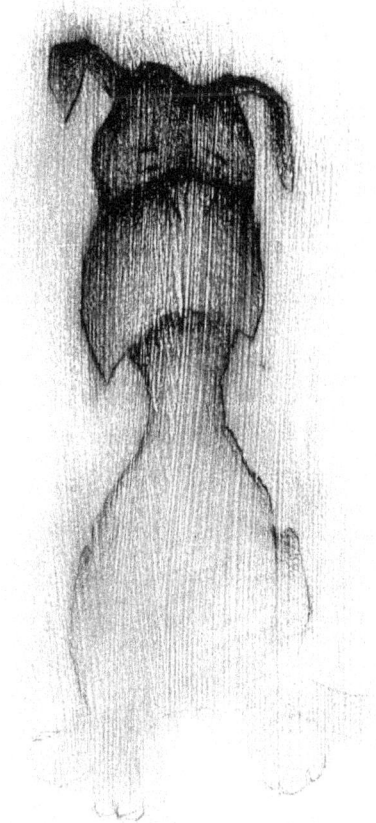

CHAPTER 8

Approaching the Edge

In April 1992, I held my breath and made my first phone call to "Bob" the psychologist, and thus started a six year professional relationship, with at least one visit per week over that period of time.

My first meetings with Bob, the counselor, involved my divulging all the details, both good and bad, of my personal history, with great emphasis on my relationships with my family of origin. I was required to do all the talking and it proved a highly emotional, hugely embarrassing experience.

There I was a mature, experienced management person, a husband of twenty years, a father, a highly educated British Chartered Accountant blubbering like a baby. All this displayed in front of a total stranger. To what depths had I fallen? What was to become of me? What did this "Bob" think of me? And on top of everything, I had to pay a professional fee for the pleasure of being humbled and embarrassed.

My first experience of "counseling" did not sit well with my image of myself... but the Black Dog was delighted.

Bob had me talk a great deal about the London blitz in the Second World War. What was it like for me to be brought up in the post-war years with all those traumatic memories that my parents had of the German bombing raids. What was it like for my parents, when they walked to St. Cuthbert's Church on a Sunday morning only to find the church lying as a pile of rubble, destroyed by a German B-1 rocket the previous night?

It is hardly surprising that Bob's first diagnosis was PTSD (Post Traumatic Stress Disorder). With the value of hindsight this was logical but incorrect.

The next step was a psychiatric evaluation, again a humbling and emotional experience but it resulted in my first ever weapon to use against the Dog. Clonazapam, a small dosage of an anti anxiety drug designed to "take the edge off an impending attack". The Dog was scowling but soon he was smiling all over his villainous face... because I would not take the medicine.

The tapes ran again, *why do you need a crutch to deal with this depression, be a man and just deal with it.* The Victorian values of "just dealing" with adversity were hard to break.

I continued to see Bob and I slowly became more amenable to the "couch/psychologist" setting. It helped a great deal in that I liked Bob personally but the reality was that I had started down the long road of learning about depression. A journey that was likely to continue to the end of my life.

About a month into my weekly sessions with Bob, I had a particularly bad attack. After consultations with Bob and the psychiatrist, it was decided that I should be admitted overnight to the psych ward at the local hospital.

If the Black Dog could talk I am certain he would have said something like, *the more this guy Dolan does to help himself, the more love and support he receives from his family, the worse it gets. And I am absolutely delighted.*

The Dog would snarl and bare his horrendous fangs. I would retreat in fear and dread of what would happen to me.

The registration process alone was a nightmare. A somewhat diffident, albeit attractive young lady asking me the most difficult, personal questions about "my psychiatric history" was another example of embarrassment to the point of my wanting to just get up, to walk out of there and drive off to who knows where. It was as if the registration took forever.

And then my wife Karen was asked to leave. I felt so alone I could just sit in the corner of the room and ask God to take me to Him.

The psych ward was on the fifth floor right at the far end of the hospital. As I walked past people, all about their own business, I was convinced that they all knew where I was going; and, of course, this just added to the stress and embarrassment. Again I asked the question of myself, *how could I have sunk this low, to need this kind of help*? I began to feel that I was entering a "prison" from which I would never emerge.

I arrived on the ward, with all the locks, double locks and security cameras. I really thought I was entering a penitentiary. Patients were standing around; some had the "glazed eyes" effect of a drug overdose. Another lady had horizontal cuts all down her forearms. Another young man was suffering fits of involuntary physical shaking. Another patient looked straight out of a "biker" movie, with tattoos covering all parts of his body, at least those parts that were visible. I was scared to death.

And as for the Black Dog... I had only seen him this delighted one time before. The Dog was so delighted that saliva was dripping from his obscene jowls.

I was "requested" to remove my belt and my shoe laces. So clutching my pants in one hand and my personal effects in the other, I was shown my room for the night.

The nurse indicated that once I was situated, I was very welcome to join the other patients for a group session. That is just what I needed; I already felt embarrassed to the point of desperation, I was scared to death, I was lonely and dreaded the thought of staying in this place.

The room was plain and, God be praised, I did not have a roommate. I got into bed and prayed that God would help me out of this dreadful place; to save me from all the addicts and other crazies I had seen on the way in: to allow me to return to Karen and my loving family just as soon as possible.

The Dog just smiled contentedly as if to say, *bring it on.*

CHAPTER 9

Downward Spiral

I awoke in the hospital bed in the psych ward, and it was a couple of seconds before I realized where I was, and then a cold sweat came over me. *Was I going to be here for the rest of my life? Was I on a path to insanity? What could I do to convince the doctors that this was all a terrible mistake?*

I was imprisoned; I was in the wrong place and should be released to my loving family immediately.

One of the many difficulties with depression is that of misinterpretation. I would invariably reach wrong conclusions when faced with a set of facts. I suppose the technical term would be in a depressed condition, my judgment would be impaired.

That is exactly what was happening to me as I woke that morning in, what should have been a safe place.

I remember laying in the hospital bed, just hoping that no one, not even my loved ones ever see me in this situation. But then as I began to assess the situation, with the help I am sure of an early morning dose of Clonaze-pam, I began to realize that the fear of the unknown was clouding any positive value to me of this experience and the availability to me of this level of expert care.

The Dog lapped up this obvious confusion in my mind and sat on the end of my bed laughing at me.

Then reality flooded my world; there was a tap on the door and my family physician, Doctor Nancy, came into the room. Dr. Nancy provided an immediate connection to the real world for me; I was so pleased to see her.

"John", she said, "it's been a bit rough this past week or so hasn't it? Karen called me to make certain I knew what was going on, but a day or so here given expert attention and you will be back on your feet."

I responded in tears, I just felt cared for and from Dr. Nancy's few reassuring words I knew that everything would somehow turn out right.

The Black Dog's expression was quizzical; he knew that he had the upper hand, but he didn't like all this support that Dolan was garnering. This was a bad place for the Dog; these medical people seemed to know what they were doing and that was threatening to the depression.

Dr. Nancy responded to my question regarding the degree of safety in this ward. Were the other patients safe to be around? I had seen sights the night before, the like of which I had never seen, even in my years of ministry. The haunting, hollow eyes; the disfigurements. The partial recovery stage from near fatal overdoses.

Nancy responded that all these folks needed medical and psychiatric care but they also needed love and nurturing. I was just the sort of person they needed in their group sessions to help them find the right direction in their lives.

With just a few words, the Dog was chastened; my spirits were raised, and I felt that I would be able to contribute positively in this situation rather than hiding away in my room, my mind filled with fear and trepidation.

An hour or so later I was in the middle of a group session, discussing some aspects of mental health care. I felt safe; I felt I was among people that understood what I was going through. The only difference was I felt their suffering was more severe than mine and they did not have the support systems in place that graced my life through family, Church and friends, but most of all the Grace of God through faith in our Lord Jesus Christ.

I remember a bizarre experience during one of the group sessions. A middle-aged lady suddenly appeared and in a loud voice asked, "Any Catholics here?" The lady was visibly ill at ease, but she had been sent on God's important business, and nothing would divert her from that mission.

Two of the group said they were Roman Catholics. At this point the visitor announced that she had brought them communion. She then instructed the two "Catholic" members of our group to hold out their hands. The visitor then thrust a communion wafer into their hands, mumbled a prayer and disappeared out of the door as fast as she came in.

I reminded myself of how afraid I was coming into the ward the previous night and reflected on the fact that "the world" had such a difficult time understanding and relating to mental health issues. How different this visit would have been if the visitor had been trained and more prepared to deal with the ways of a psych ward, and that there was nothing to fear. That we are all God's children, no matter the circumstance.

When the communion visitor arrived, for a moment I felt how I would imagine an animal felt when visitors peer at them in their cages. My friends and I, in that psych ward that day, we were the "odd ones" being visited by a well-intentioned person from the outside world.

I learned a great deal that day.

The Dog was lying quietly on the floor in the center of our circle of patients. He was not happy and from his expression clearly did not like this turn of events, particularly that Dolan was learning more about his place, and his value in the world. The Dog was to dislike what followed even more.

One of the patients asked me to stand up. She said, "I would like to introduce Reverend Johnny. Reverend

Johnny please tell us why you are here, you do not seem the kind of person that needs this kind of treatment. Have you been sent here to help us?"

What a thought, what a question to be asked. I offered a few words in response, indicating that all people have God given skills that are available and needed by others in the world. Jesus taught us that we are all here on this earth to help and care for each other. When we become preoccupied with our own problems, our own misfortune, call it what you may; it is then that we find life most difficult.

The Dog, meanwhile, had slunk away into a corner of the room and from where I sat he looked smaller. It was as if the stuffing had been knocked out of him. He was still looking at me but I sensed deep inside he was already planning a counter attack.

Just twelve hours before, I was fearful of this group of delightful people. Now they were looking to me for comfort and support. My thoughts went to the outside world and reflected on the fact that the scariest, most threatening conditions are invariably a result of human brokenness.

Love and support is the answer to all these problems. At that comment, it was as if the Dog snarled; this Dolan guy is getting too smart for his own good, I will bring him down, I will show him who the boss is, just you wait and see.

The rest of the time spent in that safe, healing place was a positive experience. My memory is of a place that, if I did have to return there, I would find it to be a welcoming, calm, healing experience.

Besides all this, the reason why I was at the psych ward in the first place, the onset of the violent anxiety attack and accompanied depression felt as if it were yesterday's news. My world had moved on.

The depression had subsided, probably in large part due to regular and effective medication in the hospital setting, I felt strong and focused and it was no surprise that the doctor released me the evening of the first day.

The Black Dog had become, small, almost inconspicuous, but while a shadow of himself just twenty four hours earlier, nonetheless he was still there.

Within twenty-four hours "Reverend Johnny" was ministering to the other patients and I began to feel reconnected to the world... I had not yet learned that the Black Dog was very much part of the total who I am; we, of course, only have one life, but to me at that time my life felt fractured.

I felt I was in the middle of a battlefield, a constant battle between good, that is my family, my spiritual and professional life, and evil represented by the Black Dog, the anxiety and depression that would creep up on me as if from nowhere and without any prior warning.

I was back to work the next day after my brief hospitalization. The hospital setting, however, had taught me a great deal, much of which I did not appreciate for a long time after the actual experience.

I learned to be comfortable in the hospital, surrounded by people suffering in a similar way to myself; back home alone it was a different story. The old feelings of fear and dread, so long established, swirled around in my head. Why did I have to go through that episode in the psych ward? Was my depression gradually worsening or was I allowing myself to accept more of the remedial therapies available to me?

What difference did the current episode make in my life? I was searching for answers.

The Dog, meanwhile, sat in the middle of the kitchen floor; he was looking brighter today and appeared larger than he did in the hospital setting. Was it the light playing tricks or did the Dog know something I didn't? I asked myself, *what more can I do, will this ever end?*

One major difference the hospital visit had made; if I felt an attack starting then I would take my prescribed medication, well at least for the time being...

With my reluctance to medication still lingering, I would take it only with the onset of an attack.

Let's get the story straight, I would take the medicine occasionally, but nowhere near the prescribed frequency.

At home... first thing in the morning, when faced with the prospect of taking the necessary medication, "the tapes" would inevitably run, oh how I wished those tapes would just shut up.

John, what have you got to be depressed about, just buck up and be a man? And men don't need the crutch of prescription drugs and all that other medical nonsense.

Nevertheless I felt there was a slight shift in my attitude. Intellectually I now accepted that taking medication was the right and responsible thing to do—it was not a sign of weakness, in fact, it was a strength to take some responsibility for my own condition.

Emotionally, however, I had a long way to go to rid myself of the tapes I had carried in my head from childhood...

CHAPTER 10

Hitting Rock Bottom

I remember the month as being November; my Mother always said that if something bad was going to happen to us as a family, it was usually in November. It was November, 1997 when I experienced the worst attack of my life.

I remember waking very early in the morning and making my way downstairs to the kitchen. I felt so beset by fear that it felt as if I was about to die. I don't remember much about that terrible time, but I do remember thinking it was too early to wake my wife Karen or the kids or call Bob, my counselor.

I felt immersed by negative thoughts; it was as if I was standing in a large water tank and water was pouring in on me. As the water became deeper and deeper, I knew I was going to drown in the waters of my own uncontrollable negative emotions.

I began to panic, but at that very moment when I feared that this might be the end of my life, I suddenly realized there was another person or entity in the water tank alongside of me.

This other person held my hand tightly and said quite clearly, I will never forget the words, *John if this is the worst that the depression can do to us, then we will both be just fine.*

The Dog stood watching through the glass of the water tank with a look of disappointment and frustration. But there was still a look in his eye that said, *John, I am not finished with you, and you will never see the back of me.* But the Dog was never the same after the water tank.

I discerned the presence of the awesome power of the Holy Spirit in that experience.

At the moment that Angel said those wonderful words to me, the water began to recede, as did my sense of fear and dread.

I climbed out of the mental water tank and from that moment forward depression began to lose its power over me.

My reflection, years later, is that the Black Dog was challenged by the Greatest Power in the Universe and the Dog lost, it was as simple as that.

The after-effects of the water tank experience were that the world looked different, and still does to this day. The terror created by the anxiety and depression lessened; the extra load in life as a result of the Black Dog gradually became easier to bear.

The experience in the water tank has been likened to the experience of Holy Baptism. A new life began for me when I emerged from the water lifted by the power of the Holy Spirit.

But let us be clear, the Black Dog did not leave my life. Given half a chance, the Dog would still take advantage of one of a "hundred" triggers. The Dog would still snarl and show his fangs: then all positive, bright colors turned a shade of gray; favorite music became tedious; my favorite people became an irritation. My creativity disappeared; it took every fiber of my being just to handle the most routine, menial of functions; those necessary just to survive.

Life would become humdrum and sedentary, only the basic needs of the day were attended to, there were no challenges, and for me that created a great emptiness in my life.

Following the water tank experience, however, the difference was that the Dog was no longer a life-threatening creature. Also the more I learned about the disease, the less power lay with the Dog, but that in no way meant the Dog had ceased to be a dark pall over my life.

I still had a long way to go to reach a peaceful life.

However, I had not only survived the worst, but had been renewed in the process.

My life settled down somewhat after the "water tank experience." The meetings with Bob, my counselor, and with my spiritual director explored areas in my life that were considered risky. "Risky" in that they were activities or events that created negative emotions and thus had a negative impact on my spiritual journey.

Events such as what some people close to me might regard as excessive use of alcohol, strained or difficult interpersonal relationships; difficult work issues, even issues with friends and the church leadership and community.

These were helpful discussions and led to a considerable amount of spiritual reinforcement. Years later I was to learn that buried in this "risky" behavior were triggers that lowered my defenses and made it easier for the Black Dog to savage me.

Again, years later I was told that for those suffering chronic depression, that certain everyday events that would normally be shrugged off, cause the sufferer's brain to go "out of chemical balance". Perspective is lost, inviting the most terrifying experiences of fear and dread. I describe these events as "triggers".

It gradually became clear to me that whereas a "normal" reaction to certain everyday events or comments would have just resulted in them being ignored; my response would be to overreact, to the point of creating the trigger for depression. This created the ideal environment for the Black Dog to move in and create havoc in my life.

At that stage in my life, however, an understanding at an intellectual level what some of the triggers were did not stifle the Dog's activities. With half an opening, the creature would still come charging at me, frequently knocking me over and standing over me with bloodlust in his eyes.

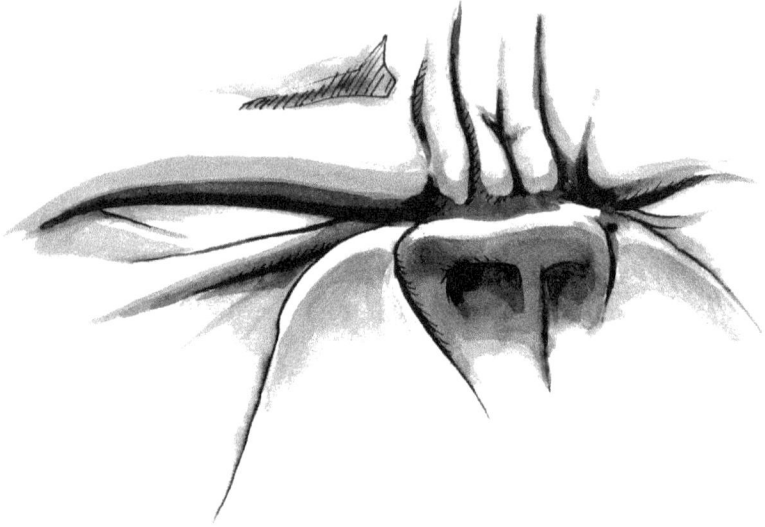

It was if the Dog was saying, albeit in a quieter voice, *So Dolan you think you have all the answers now and can control me. Just you wait and see how difficult I can still make life for you. Maybe it will be even more difficult because your understanding will increase but it won't change how you feel...*

At the very bottom of the pit, in the water tank, one moment I experienced the most terrifying feelings, but then a moment later I was in the midst of probably the most spiritual experience of my life. One moment I thought my life was ending, a split second later I felt totally safe in the arms of God.

The Dog had no say in the matter whatsoever.

The water tank was more of a "watershed" in my life.

From that point forward, depression and anxiety attacks still occurred, but they had neither the fear nor severity attached to them.

I had not yet reached the point where I was able to share this extraordinary event with anyone other than my counselor and immediate family; shame and embarrassment were still an issue.

The Black Dog, of course, thrived on those feelings and let me know on a regular basis that he may now be somewhat deflated, but the Dog, my most awful "faithful" companion, wasn't going anywhere.

I started working even harder with my counselor, Bob, on specific tools to increase my resilience to the Dog.

CHAPTER 11

The Long Climb Begins

I have always worked better with a plan. Thus I decided to create a plan to help me in my huge task ahead of me: to be free of my Black Dog. I had been given new life in being lifted from drowning in the water tank; I was determined not to waste this opportunity.

First I took an inventory of my assets; I had an immediate family that I could trust implicitly. I had Bob, my counselor, who I also trusted. Owning my own business provided me a greater choice as to whom I dealt with, and provided me the opportunity for (at least in theory) a more flexible schedule.

I have a medical doctor, Nancy, who I have always been comfortable with and who has always showed compassion toward me. Nancy never displayed any impatience toward my "invisible" illness. With Nancy I did not, and have never, felt ashamed or a fake. Dr. Nancy will be my primary doctor as long as possible in my life.

As a middle class family, we had enough resources to

be able to afford the counselor, the medication, and a comfortable standard of living.

My conclusion was that the asset side of John Dolan's balance sheet was already well equipped, but there was an even larger assemblage of liabilities.

Even after all those years of therapy, I did not fully understand why I was, periodically, struck down with this disease. What were the triggers? Why me, and why was I singled out to suffer in such a terrible way? How would people react, if I ever had the courage to share my shameful story of the Black Dog that I was unable to tame? How would they react when they learned that the strong, intelligent, successful professional and minister, was in fact a weak, self-pitying fake?

To take medication on a regular basis would just confirm the weakness in my character; also I had been overweight for years and I have been OK, so why worry about that on top of the Black Dog?

The Dog listened to my list of liabilities with a smirk on his deceptively pleasant face.

I had so much to learn, and looking back, it has taken me so many years to find at least partial answers to these questions.

The climb out of the abyss was full of promise and setbacks. The stories in this chapter will hopefully provide the reader with a sense of the uneven climb, but with the inevitable presence of the multi-faceted, supremely crafty Dog, always ready to strike and push me back into the "ravine".

In the meantime, the depression attacks continued, largely unabated. Depending on the timing of the attack, the Black Dog very easily made me seem unreliable and unwilling to meet my commitments. One particular event comes to mind; a Sunday morning and I was scheduled to preach at two services. There had been a parish event on the Saturday evening, and I had a good time, was feeling well and did not, I stress did not "over imbibe". Our pastor was at the event, and we had some pleasant exchanges. I left the party in good spirits.

That night the Black Dog attacked me with such unrelenting ferocity that when I reached the point of waking, I could not physically move, let alone call our pastor to explain my condition.

I was literally paralyzed, both physically and emotionally. I was paralyzed by fear, and by the direct effects of the disorder. My wife Karen agreed to call and explain the situation to the pastor.

"But I saw John just hours ago and he seemed fine then, how is it that all of a sudden he can't make it to church and I am left without a preacher?"

The pastor simply was unable to understand the situation based on his observation of my behavior. I had never been able to share with him my dark secret of the Black Dog. I was just too proud.

Years later, when we discussed this issue, he indicated that he had some idea that I suffered, but he had no idea of the magnitude of it.

When I recovered from the attack some ten days later, Karen and I, at the pastor's suggestion, took a sabbatical from our church. But in due course we returned to our "spiritual home", partly due to a personal tragedy that befell our pastor. To this day, the pastor and I remain good friends, and after his retirement from Church ministry, he became a professional counselor.

The former pastor and I were talking recently about what we learned from that sad time. On reflection he is the health care professional that now sees me at that time as a "high functioning depressive". This has been described in the following way:

> The patient's symptoms interact with their personalities in a way that allows them to still get on with life, although at times it is a battle that in itself has the power to bring them to an internal halt.

God works his miracles in such extraordinary ways. Even in the midst of disaster there are God's gifts to be found. As I was to discover years later, the Black Dog is always defeated in the face of spiritual strength.

In the climb out of the abyss, there were some times of inspiration as well as dark times. I recognized early on that it was necessary for me to be more physically fit in order to be able to resist the "Dog". So I joined a health club and was assigned a personal trainer, whose name was Alan Miller. I believe there are no coincidences in life: God works in His own mysterious ways.

One morning at the Health Club I was feeling particularly emotional and vulnerable. On entering the club, I observed another client using the equipment that I normally used. A minor, trivial issue for "normal" times, but in my mind at that moment, with the Black Dog urging me on, saying to me, *you show those guys*, I left the club in "a huff" and walked toward my car.

Then, for me at least, an extraordinary turn of events occurred. My trainer, Alan, his associate and two other clients all ran after me. They put their arms round my shoulders and urged me to return. I was soon to discover that Alan was only too well aware of the "Black Dog" and its deviousness, and at the vital moment he took the action necessary to break through and let me know I was important and appreciated at that place. The Dog was knocked back on his heels, completely flummoxed by this turn of events.

Later that same morning, while still at

the health club, I received a call from a parishioner, "Chertie", whose husband had been very sick and was close to death. Chertie indicated that their family were all gathered in her husband's room at the nursing home and it looked as if he was about to die.

Chertie was also worried that she did not believe her husband had ever been baptized. I was deacon on call because the Pastor was unavailable that day, Chertie asked that I come to the nursing home and baptize her husband and then read the litany for the dying.

The Black Dog was still lurking around, and I was concerned whether I would be able to honor the request. Also what water would I use for the baptism? The answer to that question lay in my hand; I would use water from the plastic bottle from the health club.

I arrived at the nursing home and found Chertie and her family members gathered around her husband's bed. The mood in the room, as one would expect, was very sad.

I requested the family members to hold hands in a circle, and I led the group through the Anglican rite of baptism. I then read the "last rites". The Dog was watching all this but he had an expression suggesting to me that he had no power to intervene.

For the second time that same day, there was an unexpected turn of events. Chertie's husband woke up, and asked what all the commotion was about and what was everybody doing there?

I cannot begin to explain the mystery of how this event

happened but I was acutely aware of the presence of the Holy Spirit in that room. The experience just strengthened my faith and the event absolutely floored the Black Dog, the power just drained from his disgusting presence.

As a footnote; three years later Chertie's husband remained alive, in a cheerful, albeit weakened condition but nonetheless responsive and alert to his life with Chertie and his family.

There were two miracles that day, the Holy Spirit saved Chertie's husband's life and our Lord removed all my symptoms of the Black Dog.

For a number of weeks I did not see the Dog.

The climb out of the abyss was full of successes and failures, but looking back, the Dog was gradually losing his iron grip on me. He could still cause a lot of discomfort, but the horrendous encounters with the fear and shame of anxiety and depression were becoming easier to bear.

But I still had a long way to go; my ability to stem the onslaught of an attack of anxiety and depression was minimal. I wasn't even convinced about the appropriateness of medication, let alone utilize other proven ways to deal with the disorder.

CHAPTER 12

The Tapes Keep Playing

I will never forget when Bob, my counselor, indicated that it was essential that I take medication to take the edge off an anxiety attack. His words were alien to me and once again I balked at the idea of using medication to ease my condition. The tapes embedded in my mind started to run again; *this depression nonsense is all in your mind and you just need to be a man, buck up and deal with it.*

The reader will recall how my family of origin, particularly my grandmother, regarded the Black Dog.

Uniformly across the family, both on our paternal and maternal sides, depression was perceived as a weakness—something shameful.

Depression was taboo, it was a subject that could not be touched with a ten foot pole, let alone be a subject for family discussion. Depression was neither worthy of compassion nor understanding. The tape continues, *John, what have you got to be depressed about, we have food on the table, you go to the best schools, you have a family that loves and cares for you; just get off the self-pity-kick and face the world the way we all have to.*

I learned early on that society, during the time I was growing up in Wales and even to this day, has a great difficulty in recognizing, let alone coping with depression. My family was the norm rather than the exception.

Depression, historically, was a mental illness, period. Mental illness was dealt with in a harsh, what these days might be considered even cruel, manner. We read that electric shock treatment was routine for "mental patients".

Lobotomies were a common procedure, leaving the patient demure but stripped of their vitality. Incarceration in mental asylums for long periods of time was probably one way in which families dealt with the shame and embarrassment of a relative suffering from depression.

No wonder that depression was not talked about. If an employer caught the slightest hint of prolonged or chronic depression, then one's job was on the line, regardless of one's position or level of responsibility. The idea of dependence on medication to deal with depression was simply unthinkable.

With this background in mind, it was hardly surprising that I was opposed to the idea of using medication to alleviate the effects of anxiety and depression.

Back at the beginning of my therapy, Bob, my counselor, had presented the idea of a medication to alleviate the negative effects of anxiety. It was to be taken in the morning "to take the edge off an attack and make me more capable of making clearer decisions as to how to manage my day".

With the advantage of hindsight, how can one produce any rational argument against the idea put forward by Bob? After discussion with my physician, the medication was prescribed for me, but the bottle of pills stood unopened for the longest time.

Then, with the onset of an attack, I began to occasionally take the medication but only under duress. The Black Dog watched and smirked that, *this guy Dolan is absurd; he gains access to a weapon that could cause me great damage and yet does not take advantage of it.*

Six years later, my boss was Mark, the chairman of the orthopedic department at The Southside Teaching Hospital in Chicago. One day our conversation moved to the medication used to treat mental health conditions. Mark was aware of my struggle with the Black Dog; he was unfailing in his support of me for many years.

Mark asked me, "Do you take medication if you have pain in your body or if you are suffering from an infectious disease?"

My answer was, "Of course."

"Then why on earth would you not take corrective medication if your brain is struggling to keep in balance, and as a result of this is giving you the symptoms of anxiety and depression?"

In face of that argument, particularly from a medical

man who I respected so much, my resistance to medication began to weaken, but I still resisted.

Even though I would not give in to the notion of medication, nonetheless, the Black Dog was not happy at this; in fact, I believe for the very first time the Dog realized he had some powerful opposition.

Out of the corner of my eye, while the dog was still large and powerful, he was also cowering and skulking off to some corner of my being.

Medication, one of the cornerstones for effective resistance against the Black Dog, was within reach, but it was another three years before prescribed medication became a daily routine for me.

I really hoped that one day medication would afford me some protection against the onset of anxiety or depression, but the old family and society attitude still clung on. *John, be a man, buck up and face your problems and deal with them like we all have to. Medication is a crutch and an unnecessary one at that.* It was so difficult for me to cut through that traditional, flawed way of thinking.

CHAPTER 13

Heavy Investment

I have already described how, in 1992, I had begun six years of weekly therapy sessions with Bob, my counselor. These sessions were invaluable in that they laid the groundwork for my future progress in coming to terms with anxiety and depression. Bob has to be one of the greatest enemies of the Black Dog, and I am sure the dog reels at the very mention of his name.

The first step in my relationship with Bob was a psychiatric evaluation with an MD. This resulted in Bob recommending medication to be available when I was faced with an impending attack. My reaction to this as I described earlier in the book was about as positive and proactive as a lead balloon.

I have described my first counseling sessions with Bob as being traumatic. In my mind's eye I saw my life up to that point as having been successful, whether it be academic, professional, my marriage and family life or my spiritual faith. But I was also very proud; and to admit the dark secret of my struggle with anxiety and depression was highly emotional and difficult for me to face.

Many tears were shed in those early sessions with Bob.

The next issue to face head on was the family investment necessary in terms of both dollars and my time in order that the counseling sessions be successful. Our health insurance would go only a short distance in covering the anticipated number of sessions, but we agreed that I needed the help and so we just plowed forward.

The therapy was to explore my emotional upbringing in great detail and gradually over the years I got a clearer picture of what this disorder was all about.

Bob and I talked a lot about the difficulty society has understanding mental health problems. Emphasis was given to the question, how can people who have never experienced the disorder first hand or never had a loved one coping with the effects of the Black Dog, how could they be expected to understand anxiety and depression?

From a sufferer's standpoint there are no rational baselines to apply to the Black Dog. It is a dreadful, painful experience; one has feelings of self loathing, of shame and embarrassment. Of appearing unreliable, the fear of what others would think if they knew about me, the fraud, the weakling, the faker.

How on earth could people who have had no experience of this disorder even begin to understand it? People would just think I was feeling sorry for myself and write me off.

I remember discussing with Bob the questions I would ask of myself. As a prime example, how would I ever hold down a job in the future if the word got out that I was mentally unstable?

I once described to Bob that I felt consumed by fear when in the throes of an attack by the Dog. We talked about those dark feelings, none of which have any merit in the light of the real world. Not to say I don't have my failings, but I have self-worth and I know I am loved, "warts and all", just as I am.

As we talked about the symptoms of an attack, I remember likening the emotional feelings to those of absolute desperation; but then gradually we began to spend more and more of our time together discussing the tools I needed to be able to defend myself from the onslaughts of the Black Dog.

Bob and D. Maria, my counselor at a later time, taught me that I needed to dump my negative thoughts in a garbage can.

I had to learn how to train my mind toward a positive, constructive path, even when under attack from the Dog. I had to learn how to "repackage" or "rearrange" my life, so that I had both the time and flexibility to better look after myself.

I talked with Bob at length about the escape routes that I had created to "hide" from the pain of the attacks. We discussed how these escape routes included socially inappropriate behaviors such as excessive drinking that would not normally be part of my everyday life; behavior that certainly did not fit in with my role as a husband, father and ordained minister.

In my discussions with Bob and D. Maria, I was never able to fully reveal the details of all these activities, or to take ownership of them. I was also never really convinced that this misbehavior was entirely attributable to anxiety and depression, but that rather the disorder might be an excuse to behave in an unacceptable, but exciting way. Whichever it was, it ended up with my having other dark secrets that I was ashamed of, and which needed to be remedied in due course for me to be free of the Black Dog.

I use the word "exciting" advisedly. It was exciting to me to have a little corner of my life that I found gave me pleasure but which put me at risk. In the light of day, as I write this text, this thinking process was nothing but absurd.

My father had a saying for this, as he did for most things. He said that everyone has spiders in their closets, but that only you know they are there. When you open the closet door to clean out the spiders, the creatures hide in even the tiniest crevice. The spiders are still there; you cannot see them, but you know you are not perfectly clean.

I believe these "exciting" secrets were perfect fodder for the Dog. I felt this voice of encouragement, *you deserve to spoil yourself after all you have been through.*

Everybody has secrets, don't worry about it. No-one, not even that darling wife of yours will ever uncover your secret; you are much too smart for that.

This devious, shameful way of looking at things simply underscores what I felt about myself when the Dog was at its ferocious worst. Clearly the devil was also heavily involved in this dialogue.

The secrets were not "escape routes"; they were additional issues to resolve if I was ever to be free of the Black Dog.

Another discussion point was that when I was under attack from the Dog, the familiar world visually changed for me. As I have described already it was if I was looking at the world through an aquarium; the lens distorted everyday sights and events so that they were harder for me to understand.

I relayed to Bob that my boss and my secretary at my place of work would tell me that they knew when I was in the throes of an attack of anxiety and depression. They said that my skin turned a "grey color" and my eyes appeared "glassy".

Bob was convinced that in my formative years, tension in my family home of origin probably contributed to the depression that appears to have wrapped itself around the asthma.

A number of great tools emerged from these years of discussion, from the weighty investment that our family was willing to make. The first and probably most valuable was I had the opportunity to share my suffering with someone outside of my immediate family and in a safe place. This taught me the value of sharing my dark secret and when I was ready to share, that the world wouldn't open up and swallow me if I said it like it is.

The second tool was that in Bob I had a backstop; someone to call and seek advice when the Black Dog came at me.

The third tool was that I began to learn from a mental health professional about the disorder itself. I learned that it was highly likely that there was a hereditary component. That my brain reacted in an "abnormal" way when faced with certain circumstances or stimuli. I have heard this termed by lay folk as a "chemical imbalance". Whatever it is, I learned it is not the way a "normal" brain is supposed to react.

I learned that the anxiety and depressive condition was manageable but not curable. In other words the Black Dog would likely always be around, maybe one day even invisible; but never completely gone. The reason of course is that the Dog is an integral part of my persona.

I learned that I was not an isolated freak—that I was one of millions of similar sufferers, many of whom would live their whole lives with this dark secret never revealed, perhaps not even revealed to spouses and immediate family members.

I learned that having anxiety and depression did not make me a bad person, but that society had a long way to go to understand what anxiety and depression was all about.

At the end of these sessions, I felt much better equipped to tackle the task, which only I could execute, that is to move down the path to recovery as far as it will take me.

The many hours of discussions provided me with clues that would mean much more to me in the years to come; clues as to the nature of the disease, but also clues as to what it would take to live a happier life having managed to harness the beast, the Black Dog.

D. Maria provided me with practical techniques that became invaluable when the Black Dog was sniffing around.

One particular tool that has been used to great effect is the image of a black garbage bag in the corner of whatever room I was in. Negative thoughts were to be consigned to this garbage bag and the bag had a seal

on it so that none of the negative thoughts could ever be retrieved.

A silver bowl stands in the opposite corner of the room; positive thoughts were available to be drawn from the bowl as replacements for the negative ones.

D. Maria helped me a great deal in convincing me how much knowledge I had that could be beneficial to other people's lives. She told me that she looked forward to our sessions, because she felt we helped each other in our objective analysis of issues. This response gave me a glimpse of an opportunity for the future; that from the experience gained from suffering all these years, I might one day be in a position where I would be qualified to help others.

As a footnote to this section, I have consulted with both Bob and D. Maria as I have written this book to make certain of my recollections and to seek their advice.

It was a proud and emotional moment to see Bob in the congregation at my ordination to become a deacon in the Episcopal Church in 1996.

CHAPTER 14

Coping Skills

Gradually I realized that if I was to enjoy a more stable and joyful life, then I needed to further develop a series of coping skills. This hopefully would provide me with the resources necessary to fight my nemesis, the beast, the Black Dog.

I believe I had matured through this difficult process, from self-pity to taking ownership of the reality of the disorder. This was a slow process and as I described in the previous chapter, it involved years of good counsel, plus I was blessed with a family who were willing to invest the money and my time away from them, to allow me to take on the challenge of long-term therapy.

I was also willing to invest the time and from somewhere

summon up enough courage to face the reality of what were the less attractive parts of my real self.

I will offer more testimony later in the book, but I would never have emerged from the nightmare of the Black Dog without the constant love and unqualified support from my dear Karen and our now adult children, Michelle Elizabeth and David John. I am eternally grateful, and I love you all more than you can imagine.

Looking back, the problem was to know where to start to build the defenses against the Dog. The idea of a plan and to take stock of my assets and liabilities, as discussed in earlier chapters, were good ideas, but that is all they were—ideas.

It seemed at times as if I was trying to climb out of a sandpit. I would make some progress in a thought process designed to beat the Dog; but then the Dog would turn on me and I would be back where I started.

Somehow I had to gain some traction to defend myself from the Dog, but it was as if what I understood intellectually was not being translated to my emotional and spiritual being. Prayer was a comfort, but I don't think I was receptive enough to hear God's answers when I sought solutions; I just seemed to be floundering.

One of the main problems was that the secret of the Black Dog remained as such; a dark and shameful secret, a secret that I had only shared with my immediate family.

But then a breakthrough, while small in itself, taught me a great deal. The Pastor of our church called me on the phone when I was in the middle of an attack.

As usual I was "hiding" from the world, not answering the telephone, and being unavailable to my family and the world at large. As my wife Karen says, in those times she would be unable to even request me to take out the garbage. It was as if a paralysis had set in.

About half an hour after his phone call, I saw a figure appear at the sliding patio door at the rear of our house. It was our Pastor, carrying two Starbucks coffees. He knocked and entered the room.

By that simple action he broke through the emotional barrier I created around myself when I was under attack by the Dog. But then I realized that it was OK and I greeted our Pastor with open arms. The world didn't close around me; I was not struck down, the world just went on as usual.

Years later, after his retirement, our now former Pastor said that I looked like the normal John. Yes I looked surprised and maybe a little shocked, but I was still the same person. My suffering was not evident to him; I just looked a little jaded.

The simple action of his not accepting the "wall" that I created around myself and caring for me enough to simply walk through it, started a process, albeit a series of "baby steps", that led me eventually to break free from this particular, so–called, defense system. The Black Dog was not at all pleased by this turn of events.

When I created this wall, I was unaware that the Dog could either remain inside the barrier or patrol the out-

side so that I could not escape. Thus the opposite result occurred than I intended; the barrier became my prison, making it more difficult for me to be rid of the Dog.

Another change occurred about that same time. The anxiety and depression attacks still occurred, but they were of a shorter duration and probably further apart in terms of frequency. This was encouraging, but I had no idea why this change was happening.

Earlier in the story, I made a comment that when in the throes of an attack, the world became distorted. As

I actively thought about developing my armory, my defenses against the Black Dog, I began to be aware of the distortion and I became unwilling to accept it.

Also, at its worst, an attack had made me feel that the whole sky was black, from horizon to horizon. No glimpse of sunlight; it was as if there was no escape from the darkness.

This perception also began to change; it was as if a black cloud was merely hanging over me during an attack, but in a relatively short time the black cloud passed on its way, allowing me to feel the warmth of the sun.

Then there was the medication issue. As I have already indicated, this was a tough nut to crack. But now, when an attack occurred I would admit the value of the anxiety medication that I had already had access to for close to ten years.

To this very day, in twenty-one minutes, the reliable medication has exactly the effect that Bob predicted all those years ago. It helps me get back on track.

The medication improved my ability to make good decisions, and thus use my skills more effectively in whatever task was at hand.

Owning my own business did not mean I was free from stress. I still had my fair share of demanding experiences. Working for my own consulting firm provided me with more flexibility, but I had to learn how to live without an automatic pay check at the end of a pay period. There were certainly times when I yearned for the prestige and stability of the executive position I had left. However that feeling soon passed, and I realized I was in a better place.

Again my wife totally supported me in the raw fact that our life would not be as financially secure as it would have been without the effects of the Black Dog. Our life, however, would be richer in other ways. I look back at that period and I see it as a time of assembling a structure from a set of building blocks. Many of the blocks were consciously learned; others were assimilated from years of counseling and discussion.

But the most important blocks were my faith in God's love and that He would ultimately save my life. I have believed for many years that our Lord needs me to do His work in the world.

I recognized that I needed to be free from the restraints that the Dog placed on me so that I might freely utilize my God-given skills.

I saw myself as making progress down the path to victory, albeit at a snail's pace, but progress nonetheless.

CHAPTER 15

Sharing and Trust

Every March, our church held a retreat at Lake Geneva, Wisconsin. The retreat was a time for study, reflection and sharing. Also a time for the renewal of long standing relationships.

The event would attract a varying number of attendees, between twelve one year to more than thirty people another. We always met at the same venue; not only the same college campus but we used the same meeting room. The majority of the attendees had signed up every year, so some of us had been to this retreat more than twelve years.

Over the years this familiar setting and a core made up of the same members of our church contributed to this venue becoming a very safe place for me.

We spent much of the retreat weekend sharing our beliefs and concerns in life. We would delve into great detail, and as a group we were good listeners.

Every year participants seemed to take more and more

risk in their opening up about their lives, but one particular year the level of trust in the small group was so strong, I was persuaded to share my darkest secret, my lifelong struggle with depression and the Black Dog.

There were stories ahead of me that stirred my heart; one young lady's story of constant sexual abuse from a relative as a child. Another story of a commodities trader caught in an FBI "sting" that resulted in him losing his wife, his home, a six figure salary, and then what felt to him like total ignominy, to have to go to work for his younger brother as a salesman.

After hearing these stories, it was easier for me to share my secret for the first time in "public", albeit to this small, intimate group. I proceeded to share the story of my longtime struggle with the Black Dog.

As I sat there, I felt my wife Karen's hand on my back, supporting me, as always, every step of the way. I shared my story in great detail, and as I talked I had mixed feelings.

I felt overwhelmed by sadness, tears welled up in my eyes; I would have preferred to be anywhere other than this place, dealing with this embarrassment.

However, I also felt something else; it was as if I felt the Dog's power being drained. I felt that maybe, at long last I had the advantage; that maybe I had the Dog on the run.

After I had shared my story I was left with a bitter aftertaste. What will people think of me now? Long established feelings of shame and embarrassment flooded into my mind. Sharing my story was almost as painful as the Black Dog itself, but those feelings were quickly put to rest.

I was amazed that many of our small group of people also had a history of struggling with depression, or they had a friend or loved one, who suffered in a similar way.

My story also paled in comparison with some of the other suffering that people had endured in their lives.

People were surprised at my story, which showed me just how well I had hidden it all these years. But my friends conveyed their admiration and respect for the fact that I was able to display my vulnerability.

The ice was now broken; my dark secret, the Black Dog, had been revealed to a selected audience in a safe place. The disclosure in itself clearly had been difficult for me and I still had mixed feelings about the risk I had taken. *Would people think less of me; was I seen as just seeking their pity? Was the Black Dog, and the attendant suffering, just a method of my gaining attention to satisfy some distorted egoistic need?*

A week or so after the sharing of the "secret", I had two principle reactions. The first was a great burden was starting to lift off my shoulders.

The second feeling was one of lingering embarrassment; I was afraid that my friends would leave the safety of the retreat setting, then, in the light of the real world they would see me as a weakling, not the strong deacon that they had, hopefully, learned to trust and respect. Time alone would reveal their reaction.

I felt it was necessary to sort out these feelings, but I also felt very strongly that in order to pull the fangs out of the mouth of the Black Dog, I needed to convey my story to a wider audience. Did I have the courage to do this, and if so, how could I achieve it? And how would others receive this baring of the soul?

What on earth would my late grandmother, Nana, think of me? She would have been disgusted by my sharing my weakness. *A Dolan has more fortitude than to grovel in self-pity. I am embarrassed for you John, for you and your family.*

The reaction of the audience at the retreat was one of admiration for my sharing, but this was not a random group. The individuals were spiritually connected in their membership of the same church. Would "the world at large" have the same reaction? Were the benefits to me important enough to warrant taking a much greater risk by broadening my audience? Yes, I decided they were.

CHAPTER 16

A Broader Audience

I decided a logical and relatively safe place to begin the process of sharing the story of the Black Dog to a wider audience was from the pulpit, where my principal motive would be to help others.

One Sunday in late 2004, I began to tell my story of the Black Dog, but as "luck" would have it, I did not feel well, and in fact detected symptoms of anxiety as I began my homily at the early church service.

I was well prepared in terms of writing the sermon and I was feeling appropriately nervous. I was at peace with myself in terms of my decision for the sharing of myself and my "darkest secret".

About half way through the sermon, out of the blue, the Black Dog began to strike me with a vengeance.

Two voices spoke to me; the Angel who saved me in the water tank encouraged me to just keep on going, that I was in a safe place and nothing bad would happen to me. The other voice was, of course, the sense of being savaged by the Dog, as if the Dog was trying to protect his domain of secrecy and mystery.

I struggled to complete my homily, feeling very badly about myself and my weakness in not being able to preach God's word from a position of strength and conviction. However, at least I was among friends who knew me and knew that I was able to do a better job. I looked out at the congregation and I suddenly saw a face I did not recognize. I felt traumatized; what on earth did this stranger think of this weak, incoherent, deacon.

With my stomach in my mouth, at least I completed my sermon in which I revealed how I had suffered from depression my whole life...

As I left the pulpit I felt nothing but bad things about myself and my feeble attempt at a message that day. I had faith that God would understand, but I felt sad that I had stumbled at my first attempt to share my darkest secret with a wider audience...

At the end of a worship service, it is custom at our church for the preacher for the day to greet the departing congregation. I received kind words from the congregation and a couple of close friends said nothing, but I knew they could tell I was struggling with the Dog.

Then the surprises started. Firstly, a few people whispered to me that they also suffered from depression, but it was a dark secret in their lives also, and how brave I was to share the information in such a forthright manner.

They also indicated a desire to talk with me more

deeply about their own experiences.

The next person in line was the face I had seen from the pulpit, but did not recognize. The lady produced a business card and introduced herself as the Pastor of an Episcopal parish in Vermont. She smiled, said that she was just visiting the area. Then she said, "Deacon John, that was the finest sermon I have ever heard from a deacon. Your intimate sharing of self and your presentation of real life issues was wonderful and you should be very proud of yourself."

I was stunned, how could I read things so incorrectly? Was this lady just being kind or did the Angel once again carry me through a bad experience? Or was I making more progress in my battle with the Black Dog then even I realized?

Whatever the answer was to that question, I didn't know, I was just confused. I was then in for another shock. In the space of a few seconds all symptoms of anxiety and depression dissolved into thin air. I felt strong and revitalized and the Black Dog appeared as a meek shadow of his former ghastly self.

Major progress was now evident to me; the power of the Dog was being diminished. The

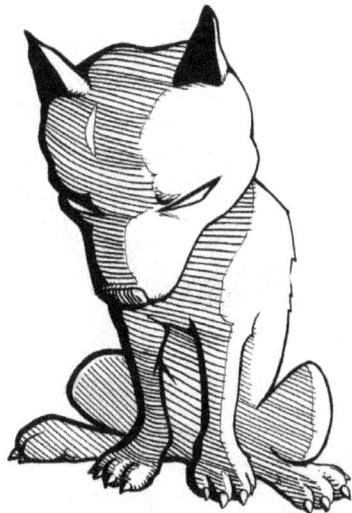

second cornerstone, the sharing of my secret, was now being put into place to cope with even the worst anxiety and depression.

CHAPTER 17

Dad's Story

One of the most rewarding features that surfaced more and more with the taming of the Black Dog is that I began to have a growing understanding and compassion for others. That I was not an aberration in the cosmos: I was not an isolated freak in this world and that there are many fellow sufferers with similar experiences to my own.

My dad was a very intelligent, thoughtful man, a man who loved his family deeply. My dad also always had an opinion, on any and all issues, and I was the recipient of those opinions, whether I asked for them or not.

The opinions did not always fall on fertile ground, and sometimes they gave rise to disputes that could develop very quickly into major conflicts. But the conflicts were of the moment, nothing lingered, other than a deep appreciation for what our dad contributed to our family life.

There existed, however, another side to my dad that I

could never really understand.

Like many homes, there was always much excitement and preparation leading up to the Christmas season. My mother always started early in her detailed preparations. My dad was part of the excitement and apprehension leading up to Christmas Eve. We invariably attended church together and my sister and I woke to the excitement of gifts and looking forward to other family members visiting for Christmas dinner and, to use a British term, to enjoy all "the fun of the fair".

But frequently dad would not rise from his bed on Christmas Day. Mom would indicate that a bad cold or flu had overcome dad and he might get up later in the day. I would make the comment, "But he was OK last night."

Mom would answer, "You know your dad!"

The point was I thought I knew dad, but I didn't, at least not in those situations.

When dad was sick and separate from us, I would creep into his bedroom and dad would be sleeping, almost hidden under the bedclothes.

This made my sister, Lizzie, and me sad for dad to be missing, but I remember this as not an uncommon experience.

The same thing would happen around my dad's birthday or the day after we arrived at a vacation destination, particularly when we visited my dad's mom, "Nana". Dad would suddenly be subject to a mysterious ailment, which would keep him in bed and unavailable to the family.

I could never understand it: I missed my dad and felt sad when this happened, but like everything in life I guess, I got used to it.

Then there were the weekends at home when dad would literally become a hermit. He would be working in his greenhouse or would be chopping firewood, usually in the garage.

Sometimes a work commitment came out of the blue and he would be gone for most of the waking hours over a weekend.

This "strange and quiet dad" was most noticeable when we were with Nana. Immediately when we arrived at Nana's house, usually after a five hour car journey, with, of course, limited or no access to a telephone in those days, my dad would be chastised by Nana for arriving at a time different from that which was forecast.

My Dad would never argue with Nana, but he would arrange a whole list of appointments that would take him out of the house. A visit to the barber shop, even if he had his hair cut just days before. He would go on errands to the hardware store or to the newsagents. He would go shopping with mom which would never, ever, happen at home.

Then he would have a day or two with the onset of a "mysterious cold", much the same routine as at Christmas time at home.

Dad would never utter a word of criticism of anybody; he would not be angry. He would just be quiet and

unavailable; he would not be like my real dad, and it made me feel sad.I could never understand it, I just got used to it.

In 1959, dad "decided" to go to Malaysia to work with the Telecommunications Department of the Malaysian Government. As I remember it, this assignment was under the aid provisions of the United Kingdom Government and the United Nations. Dad had clearly discussed it at length with our mom, but I remember it as a surprise. Furthermore my mom and sister were to join dad after a few months, but I was to stay home.

Since our home was to be rented while they were gone, it was arranged that I stay with a school friend of mine. I was seventeen years old.

On one hand I felt excited at my impending freedom. On the other hand I felt lonely and sad. Later my dad was to explain that either we had to move from Wales or he took the posting which would allow him to save some money and give us all some new experiences. I still felt sad and lonely, and I really didn't fully understand why I was to be left alone.

I never really understood why dad would plan to leave us at that time.

In 2007, just five years ago, twenty-six years after my dad's death, my late friend and mentor, my Uncle Vernon talked with me. My Uncle Vernon, then ninety-three years old, had kept a secret for more than eighty years, but felt that it was time that I knew something important about my dad.

When Uncle Vernon was just ten years old and my dad was fifteen, my dad shared a secret with his brother, Vernon, that no one else in the world would ever be aware of.

Dad swore Uncle Vernon to secrecy, because if the truth came out, my dad thought, probably correctly, that he would be seen as weak, unreliable, and vulnerable to predators at work and in many other places in society.

My dad suffered his whole life from his own Black Dog. As Uncle Vernon described it, it was a carbon copy of my own suffering; the only difference being that dad suffered his whole life without medication, without counseling and without the loving understanding of a mother, spouse and family.

My dad's only recourse was to be away from everything and everyone and suffer in silence.

As my Uncle Vernon related this story to me, the Black Dog, small and shriveled, just sat and listened. He was being put in his place in the reality of the world and was now becoming even less powerful.

But I still a perceived a slight mean look in the Dog's eyes; given half a chance, he would still make me and my growing family's lives a "bloody" nightmare.

I wished my dad was still here for me to discuss it with him, but I know he is living in my heart for all time and that he knows how I wish I had been able to help him. I would also love to ask him, did his battles with the Black Dog contribute to his decision to go to Malaysia?

When my dad was close to death at age seventy-one years, he made the comment to me, that he "had passed the God-given three score and ten years, and it was time for him to be at peace". I ask myself now, was dad alluding to his private struggles with the Dog and was he just tired?

I know how difficult anxiety and depression can be, but in my life I have been blessed with emotional support, I have acquired an increasing understanding of the Dog and I have accepted and am using the appropriate medications and other weapons necessary to tame the creature.

Dad was on his own. It must at times have made his life intolerable. Also our beloved dad, the "tower of strength" in the family, was as vulnerable as any of us.

God Bless you, dad, for all you did for your family, your church, your career in spite of, and in defiance of the Black Dog.

It is hard for me to believe that there are fellow sufferers in the world as close as one's own parents, who hold to themselves the dark, impenetrable secret of the Dog... even unto death.

CHAPTER 18

Medication

It was a great shock, and I felt very sad on learning of our dad's suffering, without any relief through medication or being able to share his own dark secret with anyone except his kid brother Vernon.

Dad was raised in a society and family community that were clearly afraid of mental health problems. This fear presented itself in a total intolerance for any illness or condition that did not fit into the norm and which could not be readily explained at a physical level.

Knowing how my dad must have suffered without any tools to fight his Dog, helped remove my last objection toward accepting the concept of regular, ongoing, medication. I now saw medication as the next cornerstone in my defense system against the Black Dog. It is a wonderful thing that my loving dad was still able to help me more than thirty years after his death in 1981.

My resistance to medication is fully described earlier in this book. I have commented that it made no sense intellectually, but the old tapes still ran in the back of my mind.

However my resistance was getting much less and in 2004 I found it not just acceptable, but a very positive move to take medication on a regular, preventive basis.

Another defensive cornerstone at last was in place, which has really helped to balance out any negative effects of the Dog.

I discussed the issue of medication with my Family Doctor, Dr. Nancy. We then started on the journey to find the right combination to deal with both anxiety and depression.

Dr. Nancy's patience, her attentiveness and persistence helped me on this search for the right combination of drugs, but it took more than a year to find the right answer, the right balance.

Five years later these medications continue to work wonders for me.

Since that point of time, I have built the medicine into my daily routine, so that I never miss. Also I am not reluctant to take extra doses, so long as that conforms to my doctor's orders.

It took me a long time to get to this point, but I also have no thoughts of "weaning myself off the medication".

From a spiritual perspective, God has provided humanity with the knowledge to invent medication in response to aberrations in our human physicality.

That is sufficient argument for me.

Thank you Bob, D. Maria, Mark, Dr, Nancy and others who attempted to educate me earlier, but now "I have got it".

Better late than never.

CHAPTER 19

Triggers

For many years, I have been committed to spending a lot of time learning about the Black Dog and not being afraid of facing up to my enemy.

I believe, however, that I have also had the strongest possible ally through this process. The same hand that came to my rescue when I was drowning in the water tank has been a constant supporter and companion.

Jesus Christ has been and is with me with every step of my journey.

With my now taking medication on a routine basis, the Dog faces a line of defense that is getting stronger every day. It is only in recent years that I have not just been learning the value of coping skills, but actually creating and honing them.

I was beginning, at last, to actually experience the enormous value in being able to anticipate and ward off attacks of anxiety and depression.

I was now able to share the details of depression with

friends; I also had learned how to control my feelings so as to avoid the foul aftertaste of shame that accompanied my early experiences with sharing my story of suffering from depression.

Now I was able to rationally turn my mind to those people and situations that traditionally acted as triggers; to plan how I was going to deal with them.

In the six years of therapy with Bob and later with D. Maria, I had learned a great deal about anxiety and depression. I felt it was in my power to cope with this condition given the right tools, but that I could not do it without the tools.

I drew from an abundance of wise advice from these two, skilled professionals. One of these pieces of advice; there will always be information or news that is unpalatable to you. In your mind always have a figurative, garbage bag in the corner of the room. Place anything or anyone in that garbage bag if you know that it/they will act as a trigger. By doing this, you exercise power over personal feelings that might get exaggerated or distorted and result in harm to you by weakening your defenses, and thus allowing the Black Dog to attack.

The first situation, and probably the most powerful trigger, is if I feel unappreciated. It is also the most difficult to deal with. Serving a church community as a deacon means living a life of unconditional contribution to other people's lives. One does not look for appreciation; one is fed spiritually by the selfless act of giving, but more on this in later chapters.

The second trigger is how I react to surprising news or events. This is the hardest to understand because it almost depends on my emotional mood at the time. My reaction to such stimuli in a normal, healthy frame of mind is to brush the issue off or put it aside and move on with life. But when the Black Dog is sniffing around, my reaction exaggerates the information, always toward the negative.

Coping with this is probably the most difficult, but I have now developed techniques. In the movie "A Beautiful Mind" we learn about the life of John Forbes Nash Jr. and how he used his mind to control his schizophrenia. I learned a great deal from Mr. Nash's story.

Certain people can be a trigger for the onset of anxiety and depression, particularly people who I instinctively do not trust. A trigger, also, is when people disappoint me but I treat the disappointment as if it didn't matter, which is not really how I feel.

Transitions, particularly from one role to another, can be a trigger; I will always remember having a delightful weekend with my wife, Karen, in Washington DC. On the Monday, I was scheduled to attend a conference and late Sunday afternoon, Karen flew back to Chicago.

The Black Dog savaged me that week. I was alone; I did not know many people and I missed my wife. The ideal ingredients for an attack, and I was not disappointed!

Years ago, I remembered being in my dad's car as he gave me a ride to school after I had been sick at home with asthma. I was transitioning from a sick, vulnerable child to an individual seen as bright, competent and "one of the boys" at school. The thought of this transition was too much to deal with. I feigned illness at the time but, in retrospective, I was suffering an anxiety attack.

The holidays, particularly Christmas, can be a powerful trigger because the holidays bring with them historical reference points and the "tapes" start running in my head. All those years ago, my dad exhibiting his own difficulty with holidays had a deep effect on me because I loved my dad and missed him when he was absent from festive occasions.

A friend of mine, some fifty years ago, said to me, "The day will come when, John, you will no longer need to feel you have to be such a large guy." All those years ago I believe my friend, Chris Hill, was talking about my physical weight, and the psyche attached to it.

The day when I no longer felt I needed to be a large man has arrived for me on a number of occasions over the years, but it also left me the same number of times. I am left with a constant battle with weight that has had a derogatory effect on my physical health for many years.

Poor physical health in itself has also been a trigger for the onset of the Black Dog. Other triggers certainly exist, high stress levels and dark, cloudy days, and there were certainly enough of those growing up in Wales.

CHAPTER 20

Resilience

There has been great value in my developing a thorough understanding of the triggers that are precursors to attacks of anxiety and depression. However, I also have had to learn how to respond more effectively to the circumstances that would precipitate the release of the Black Dog.

I learned that these responses are at cognitive, emotional, and spiritual levels. I have had to learn how to respond at all three levels.

Let us examine each of the triggers and how I have been able to acquire resilience.

In order for me to understand why I would consider myself "unappreciated", it was necessary for me to develop a clearer understanding of my relationship with the world. I am blessed to have learned a relatively simple fact; I know even within my own family of origin that others do not appear to have learned this throughout their whole lives.

The simple fact is that the world does not revolve around me, John Dolan. I have learned that those other people, the so-called "unappreciaters" have their own priorities, concerns and issues to deal with in their own lives. John Dolan, his issues and sensitivities are certainly not automatically the number one agenda item in other people's lives.

If a person I am dealing with seems distracted, or in any way seems disinterested in my agenda, that does not automatically mean they do not appreciate my contribution to whatever we are dealing with.

If a person fails to greet me with a smile or does not say "good morning", it does not automatically mean that person does not appreciate me or is against me. It may merely indicate that the particular person is distracted by other events in their lives.

This may not always be the case; there may well be times when an individual is blatantly rude or inconsiderate. I am still learning that I am not the universal judge of good manners; that sometimes one should confront the issue, but generally it is best to just ignore the issue, to pray for that person, and to move on down the road.

At my age and circumstance, I believe these are just the true facts of life. I try harder to be more circumspect when faced with a situation where I feel "unappreciated". I have learned to simply accept people for where they are in their own lives, without assuming that their attitude has anything to do with me or my behavior.

I have learned techniques for dealing with potentially negative or disturbing news. The first is that I control when I respond to the information; there are few situations, other than legal demands, that require an immediate answer.

Historically, I would always feel it was my responsibility to deal with the issue immediately; my knee jerk reaction was not nearly as considered nor effective than if I had "breathed in three times", and only responded after I had given myself sufficient time to properly consider the issue.

My spontaneous response would inevitably be accompanied by a welling up of negative emotion in my gut. My imagination would always create the worst possible scenario arising from the news.

I have learned that a more paced, considered response gives time for the emotions to calm down. Also, I invariably consult others about how I should respond to the news. My wife, Karen, is highly skilled in this particular area, and has taught me a great deal in how to respond to situations one has not anticipated.

An example presented itself as I wrote this text. I had specifically requested a certain role in an upcoming church event and I then learned I was appointed to, what I considered at the time, a "lesser" role. My immediate reaction was to be chagrined and not needed, but more telling was the familiar rise of indignant emotion; I could feel it in my stomach.

I talked the issue through with Karen. I "slept" on it

and the next day I just felt honored to serve in any capacity. Any negative feelings flew right into the symbolic black garbage bag familiarly placed in the corner of the room.

In terms of specific persons acting as triggers; as early as 1993, from my traumatic experience at the medical group, I determined a link between certain person's actions and the onsets of anxiety attacks and depression.

I talked in previous chapters about the physician we will call Patrick, who made my life at the Southside Medical Group extremely difficult. But I learned later on that he had a well developed reputation for his "abrasive" behavior, and he certainly rubbed me the wrong way. It was some small comfort to know that others suffered from his double dealing and sharp tongue.

It was not just Patrick, I was working in a pool of uncontrolled physicians' egos, and if things went well, I was respected, even lauded. However when business affairs turned south, John the "star" quickly turned into John the "dog".

The other dog, the Black Dog, was of course delighted with that situation.

Over the years, I have been fortunate to be able to become much more selective as to whom I work with and who I trust. I believe I have a well-developed sense of who I can rely on, so that if I follow my gut sense, then this in itself offers me great protection from the Dog. On occasions, I inevitably will make a bad choice, but I have also developed sounding boards before I make the choice to allow a person to get really close to me.

My immediate family, Karen, Michelle and David, prove invaluable to me over and over again in this regard. Also, there is a group of Christian men friends that I have breakfast with twice a month.

We have met as a group for more than six years. Vance, Harry, Peter and I share concerns and questions with each other and we have developed an implicit trust in each other that is truly a blessing and an iron-clad defense against the Dog. I have never experienced the presence of the Black Dog in their company, either individually or as a group.

There are also other friends and colleagues both within the church and the broader community that similarly serve as faithful council. At the very top of this list are three men.

Firstly, my friend and my attorney for more than twenty-five years, Alexander (Sandy) Kerr. I owe much to his pragmatic, clear, thoughtful advice on so many issues. Frank Nicholson, my mentor and friend for more than forty years, and my friend for almost fifty-five years, Nigel Calder from Llandaff, Wales. I trust these people with my life and will always be indebted to them for creating stability out of a crazy world. Their influence and sound judgment has been a tower of strength for me in my battle with the Black Dog.

I believe, with God's help, I have largely solved the problem of individuals being a trigger for anxiety or depression.

Transitions from one role to another are still difficult for me; but the Black Dog can be stifled by my talking with trusted others about the transition and what is involved in that transition. Also to always be well prepared when it comes time for making the change in role and/or situation.

I believe this is one area where those unfamiliar with the wiles and tricks available to the Black Dog can only sit and scratch their heads. How can something so simple for the "average" person become so complex for those who suffer from anxiety and depression?

I have found that it is vitally important for me to be in the right frame of mind when making transitions. Prayer and meditation as well as exercise feature prominently as valuable tools to help me be mentally prepared.

The following scenario illustrates how this problem still impacts me on a day to day basis; however it also describes the techniques I have learned to deal with the issue. A few weeks ago I was invited by my daughter to have lunch with her and my grandchildren. I had an early business meeting that same morning; I put on my first hat of the day. Then I led the midweek service at our church which involved a short sermon; a second hat.

Then came another transfer, from the role of cleric to father and grandfather, thus wearing a third hat. Then came a transfer from father and grandfather to my being a disgruntled customer at a local store, where I had to resolve a dispute involving perceived poor service by the store; my fourth hat.

Finally, the transition from the store dispute to being a loved and loving husband, my fifth hat of the day.

I enjoy four of these five roles and situations but I serve in a different role in each setting, and I have learned that if I have discomfort in the transitioning of these roles, then it creates fertile ground for the Black Dog to strike.

This particular morning, my schedule meant that I arrived at my daughter Michelle's house earlier than scheduled. Rather than sit and sulk that I was not important enough for my daughter to be on time, I sat on their porch, in a wooden rocking chair, enjoying the quiet and the freshness of early spring, the birdsong and the color and fragrance of the flowers in their yard.

A couple of neighbors were out walking and jogging in the cool air; pleasantries were exchanged and I felt at peace, looking forward to my loved ones arriving home.

The visit with my daughter, Michelle, and my grandchildren was one of the most relaxed and joyful times I have ever spent with them.

It should be no surprise to me that others fighting their Black Dogs share the same feelings regarding transitions.As I have stated repeatedly through this book, the greatest ally the Black Dog has is the sufferer's reluctance to share concerns with others. This conscious sharing is the single most effective healing action, but to the sufferer I believe it is the most difficult.

This is the first time I have ever elaborated on my

difficulty with transitions, but I have learned much by this description and through this testimony; the Black Dog has just lost even more influence.

The holidays, a time for celebration and family interaction are still a time of vulnerability for me. But again, unlike my dear late dad, my immediate family is aware of my sensitivity to the Black Dog rearing his head in such settings.

I have learned not to have unreasonable expectations, high or low, from family gatherings. I have also learned that a better time is frequently had by all if we meet, as a family, on "neutral territory". A rented house in Galena or an apartment on the Spanish island of Mallorca are examples of this.

I have learned that there are danger signals which, when read, can thwart the Black Dog: excessive use of alcohol and obsessions about family foibles, unusual manners or idiosyncrasies among the wider family, that are unusual or different from how our immediate family behaves.

Historic grudges and irritations have a habit of showing their "heads" at family events. I have learned that discussion of these "danger signals" ahead of time, and how we are to deal with them, removes the sting of surprise from the Black Dog.

Over the years, I invariably would fall into one or more of these potholes resulting in the Black Dog rampaging through the event and damaging me and my family's enjoyment of family gatherings. However, over the years, besides understanding my vulnerabilities, I have developed techniques to minimize or remove the Black Dog.

The most frequent pothole I have "visited" over the years has been alcohol, but I now enjoy the assistance of some reliable "lookouts" in my immediate family.

My struggle with excessive physical weight and its negative impact on my general physical health has been a trigger. As an adult, what should be the simplest discipline, to control my weight, has proved very difficult for me.

In writing these words, once again I make a commitment to myself, my family and my friends that I will embark on a suitable diet and exercise regimen that must lead to improved mobility and my physical health.

Failure to properly manage daily stress of life is a trigger, but dealing with daily stress is an integral part of being fully alive. Hiding from the world is stressful. Escaping to an exotic hideaway is stressful, or at least "they" tell me. Overwork is stressful, as is too much travel, as is too little work.

I believe part of answer to the issue of stress is moderation in all things, but also consciously turning the stress over to God. God can handle stress much more effectively than we ever can.

I can't do much about dark, cloudy days. Oh, yes I can; I can obtain a full spectrum lamp for my office that reproduces the effect of sunlight, replenishes the body's vitamin D and reduces the influence of the Black Dog.

I did that one time, and I ended up after about a month of use, with a major suntan on the top of my, albeit balding, head.

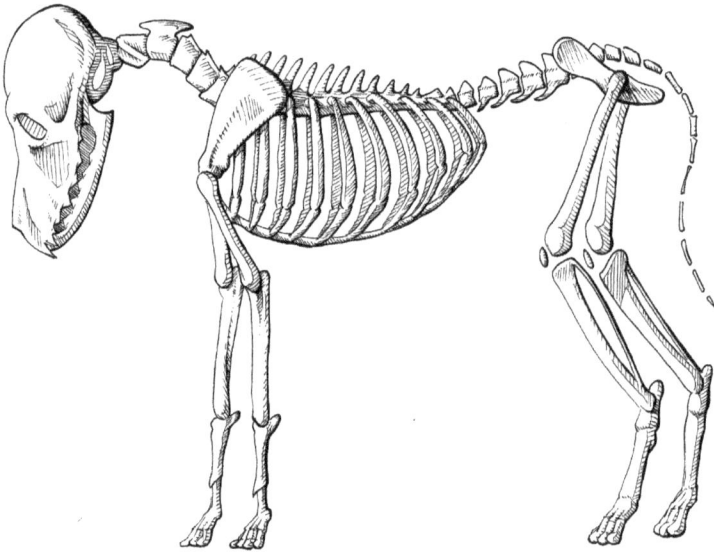

With all this information now helping me to develop resilience to anxiety and depression, I am not yet rid of the Black Dog. However the Black Dog represents himself as a very different image than years ago.

Frequently now I see the dog as a mere living skeleton. It is as if a strong rush of wind will just blow him away.

CHAPTER 21

Thinking of Others

One of the most undesirable features of chronic anxiety and depression is that there is only room in one's thinking for one person; and that person is you, the sufferer. All one's thoughts are focused on survival; fighting the Black Dog with any weapon at one's disposal. The longer the attack lasts or the more severe the attack, the more one retreats into oneself.

My experience was that the Black Dog would strip me of my sense of humor and my creativity. It would separate me from the personal characteristics that I enjoy the most. The Black Dog would diminish my skills and attributes that I used to connect with others in the world. One result of this disconnect was that I became desensitized to others' concerns and needs.

It took all my energy and focus to survive; there was just no ability to even consider other's feelings. It must have been a nightmare for my loved ones.

In moments of extreme sadness and frustration, my

wife Karen would say, "Where's my Johnny? All I want is the man I love and who I married, to be back with me."

The Black Dog caused a whole dimension of my life to close down. Anticipation and excitement associated with planned events would disappear into the fog and despair of my depression. I was not even aware of the negative impact on my loved ones, particularly my spouse.

When burdened with the Dog, I would misinterpret an innocent comment; a look or an innuendo or a gesture would be misconstrued. This must have made a loved one's life very miserable. It was also very difficult for my friends and colleagues, but I would hide away from people outside the immediate family so they were largely insulated from the change in my persona.

Probably one of the most significant facts described in this book is that I recently asked my very best friend, Karen, "would she have married me if I had been burdened with depression at the time when we met and in our early years when the children were born"? Her answer was that she remembers indications of the Black Dog early in our relationship but she was committed to our being married no matter what!

One of my most treasured possessions is a simple glass paperweight that sits proudly on my desk. It is engraved with the word "soul mate", together with the definition, "a person for whom one has a deep affinity, especially a lover, wife, husband etc."

Karen's commitment was to her soul mate. While the impact of the black Dog was very painful for her, so can many other illnesses and conditions of life.

We are a partnership and that is how we have learned to approach difficulties that inevitably arise from time to time.

As I began to effectively use my coping skills, my mind gradually was able to turn toward my loved ones and how much they had also suffered at the times of my attacks. Their sense of helplessness and loss when their husband, their father, became a "gray shadow" of his normal self must have been very painful.

As my coping skills became more effective, the frequency and severity of attacks by the Black Dog lessened. For the most part, life slowly began to become more normal.

Besides a calmer, more predictable life, what emerges most from this chaos is a huge sense of gratitude, of respect and of admiration for Karen, my wife and Michelle and David, our offspring, and how they dealt with the situation.

During the worst years, my family were all busy in their own lives. My wife had her own demanding career as a Licensed Clinical Social Worker. Our kids were both very active in high school and they tell me it was not as if they were at home experiencing the full impact of my situation.

As the attacks became less, the dog ceased to be such a major presence in my life. If it was present, it was a mere shadow of what it had been.

I was now able to accept that the dog was simply part of my persona. It was how I was genetically wired and how I was emotionally disposed. It didn't dominate me or create fear in my mind. I was conscious of its presence, but I had become resilient to the point of being able to think of others ahead and outside of my own concerns for survival.

It has been said to me that one positive outcome of my struggle with my black dog is that my level of compassion for others' problems has developed proportionately. I am able to be more available for others, my family and friends foremost, but also to others in the world who are in need of love, compassion, and practical help.

It is said that time is the great healer. As the distance between attacks becomes greater, I have started to forget the emotional horror of the experience when battling the Black Dog. Intellectually, the memories are still there, but I have faith that in due course the memories will take a back seat in my life, to be replaced with concern and compassion for my family and the growing number of people who rely on me as their husband, father, grandfather, relative, friend and deacon.

Compassion and concern for others is filling the void created by the diminished black dog, but I still expect, and do experience "bumps in the road".

This past Thanksgiving Holiday, I received all the warning signs of an impending attack. But I did two things; I shared the feeling with a friend, albeit by text message, and then I took additional, prescribed, medication.

In the space of twenty minutes, the negative feelings waned and I was able to immerse myself once again in family matters, joys as well as concerns.

There are also some scars that still need healing; I referred earlier to the negative impact on our daughter when I used alcohol to excess as a means of escape from the Black Dog. To this day, Michelle is insistent that I do not drink to excess in family gatherings, because she wants to be with her dad, not some alcoholic distortion of the dad she knows and loves, and now the Papa that our grandchildren know and love. I have learned that is just one of the many ways that Michelle shows she loves her dad.

The coping skills I have learned repeatedly prove themselves valuable in my life. They have transformed my existence so that I can now lead a "normal" life and in turn be available for concerns and issues that affect my friends and loved ones.

I am deeply grateful for the love and unqualified

support provided by my immediate family during the times of my battles with the Black Dog.

I now have a deep appreciation for my family's shared suffering when I was unavailable or in some way altered by my condition. In so many ways I wish the Black Dog had never existed, but I also know how much sensitivity I have acquired as a result of my suffering.

CHAPTER 22

Coaching from One Human's Experience

We are now approaching current times in my story, and I would like to discuss perhaps the most important value that emerges from my years of fear, of pain and dread. That value is my ability to share my story with others; not just the painful parts, but the joy of having emerged from the grasp of the black dog. The power invested in me so that I am now able to coach others about the condition and how to address a remedial? condition.

I wish to state very clearly that I am not and do not purport to be a qualified counselor. However, I am an ordained minister with more than sixteen years' experience in pastoral care. But even more important is the fact that I have been there; I know what the hell is like of suffering from chronic anxiety and depression. I am able to state with authority that there is hope for the sufferer—that we all can have the tools available to us to prevail over the black dog and live calm, comfortable, productive lives.

Of all the coping skills developed over the years, I think the most valuable is being able to share my story with others without it leaving a bad taste in my mouth. I am not embarrassed or ashamed of my battles with the Black Dog. It is all part of me and how I was made, and a result of the influences on me during my life.

I am not angry or resentful for having to deal with my anxiety and depression. In fact, I regard it as a gift from God that I have learned, with God's help, how to cope, which now puts me in the position of being well qualified to help others in their own battles.

This book itself is offered as a message of hope to the millions of people out there who suffer in some similar way from anxiety and/or depression.

Many fellow sufferers feel that they are unique; freaks in a world that does not understand, let alone tolerate the Black Dog.

I have been given the opportunity and privilege to let those dear souls know that they are not alone and that they have the opportunity to tame the Dog. This was the principle reason for writing this book, to let others know that they are not alone, and that recovery techniques can be learned from the right teacher.

I would like to describe one example of this. In an earlier chapter, I described a situation where my personal trainer, Alan Miller, was sensitive to my feelings to the point of pulling me out of a growing conflict with the Dog.

Well, after a few months of working with Alan, he shared with me his own terrible experience with his own Black Dog. Alan's upbringing and situation is very different from mine, but the symptoms of our battles with our Dogs are eerily similar. Alan is a young man in his early thirties.

Alan has a long way to go in his journey with the Black Dog, but he is in therapy, has accepted medication and is much further advanced than I was at the same age.

Alan and I have spent countless hours comparing notes and I believe we have helped each other a great deal.

During the planning stages for this book, we, in fact, explored collaboration between the two of us in writing our stories in parallel in this volume. Our conclusion was that, while both our intentions are similar to write our stories to help others in the world, nonetheless there is just too much information to fit neatly together in one book.

I discuss this more in the epilogue to **The Black Dog**.

There are of course many people, some in the most unlikely of professions, who just cannot or will not consider the effects of anxiety and depression as being real. I am sure in many cases that there are good reasons why they are intolerant or dismissive about the mental health condition.

Family experience or just a "blind spots" do not allow them to offer solace to those who genuinely suffer. Sometimes I believe the hardest people to convince are those who themselves are silent sufferers. To admit that the condition is valid and that many others struggle with their own Black Dogs is just too painful to consider.

I feel so sad for those, like my dad, who are forced to suffer in silence. Also, I pray for those who could not bear the pain and suffering any longer, and are no longer with us in this world. I feel particularly sad for those dear souls because there is an alternative to their pain and suffering, which I have been so fortunate to have found in my life.

There is an alternative life available to us, but it requires hard work, good professional counseling, and investment of time and money. It also requires the love and devotion of one's family and, most importantly, the presence and power of the love of God.

CHAPTER 23

A Time of True Testing

My first major health problem emerged a number of years ago, but its resolution remains hard to explain, at least medically.

In 2006, I was diagnosed with hypertension, i.e. very high blood pressure, and I had been under the care of a cardiologist for about a year. Little or no progress had been made even though I had endured numerous tests and medications.

The Black Dog was in his element; he loved the floundering and the uncertainty associated with the treatment of my condition. I suffered accordingly. One day the cardiologist put his arm on my shoulder and my lay interpretation for what he said was, "John, you are a mystery and I am not exactly sure what to do next."

Well, I knew what to do next, I requested my primary physician, Dr. Nancy, to change my cardiologist, and so I was referred to and met Dr. Robert.

My first appointment with Dr. Robert lasted over an

hour. During that time we explored the health issues of my family of origin; but even more importantly it appeared to me that Dr Robert taught me much of what he knew about my health issue. He taught me how I could become his partner in managing my condition.

The dog was present at that meeting but he appeared small and emaciated, and if it is possible he had almost a scared expression on his face.

Eventually Dr. Robert identified that I was likely suffering from the same condition that had killed my dad in 1981. However, he added the caveat that healthcare in the 21st century had tools available that weren't even dreamed of in 1981.

In a matter of weeks, the medication prescribed by the good doctor had reduced my blood pressure to normal. Some twelve months later I was able to be taken off all blood pressure medication.

In April 2011, I attended my six month check-up with Dr. Robert. He showed me a recent letter he had composed and sent to my primary physician based on my most recent tests. The hypertension had disappeared, and Dr. Robert was unable to give a complete medical explanation. In the letter he characterized it as "unexplainable internal combustion that had corrected my condition".

My conclusion is that the Angel, present in the water tank all those years before, had been working very hard with Dr. Robert and myself to heal me.

A tiny dog sat in the corner, confused and ineffective.

The first test highlighted the diminished power of the dog!

In the following two years, I was to be severely tested by three major events in my life. Each of these events, historically, would have resulted in severe battles with the black dog.

In 2010 and in 2011 I suffered from a number of significant health problems, two of them resulting in my being admitted to the hospital.

In September 2010, I was admitted to the hospital, virtually unable to breathe on my own. I was suffering from pneumonia. My friend Nigel travelled from our home village in Wales to be with my wife and I. My family and friends were very concerned about my prognosis.

I can truly say from the moment I was in my car being driven to the hospital, right through the hospital stay, through the period of recuperation, there was no evidence of the presence of the black dog. In the dog's place was a sense of well-being and of being in a safe place with people I love and trust.

I felt safe and at peace in the care of my family and friends, the doctors and nurses, and in the arms of a loving, caring God, who has helped me to this place of joy in my life. More close to home, Nigel's daily visits to the hospital gave me a great boost at a critical time; and with his Welsh humor, he soon had the nurses asking when he would be returning.

About six months after the first hospitalization, I found myself, as the Deacon, conflicted at a spiritual level with the new Pastor of our Church.

In order to protect my physical and spiritual health, I decided it was necessary for me to move on from the Church where I had been a member for more than thirty-one years. This would have been a perfect occasion for the dog to complicate matters. There was absolutely no sign of the dog.

The third event was major emergency surgery while my wife and I were vacationing with our son, David, and his family in Southern California in July 2011.

I was hospitalized for almost two weeks and then spent another month, recuperating at our son's home until such time as I was able to fly home to Chicago.

Five hours of intensive surgery saved my life; I am told it will take me about twelve months for my body to fully recover from the rigors of that amount of surgery.

Once again through the whole experience, I have seen no sight of the black dog. I have not even suffered from the expected post-surgical depression, a frequent occurrence even for the most robust of patients.

The black dog has been replaced with a sense of peace; a sense of well-being, of being safe and protected.

The message from this time of testing is that my defense mechanisms to thwart the black dog work: faith and hope, knowledge of the condition provided by many hours of counseling, the right balance of medication. The ability to freely share my concerns with others; the ability for not isolating myself from others, particularly loved ones. All these coping skills did their job.

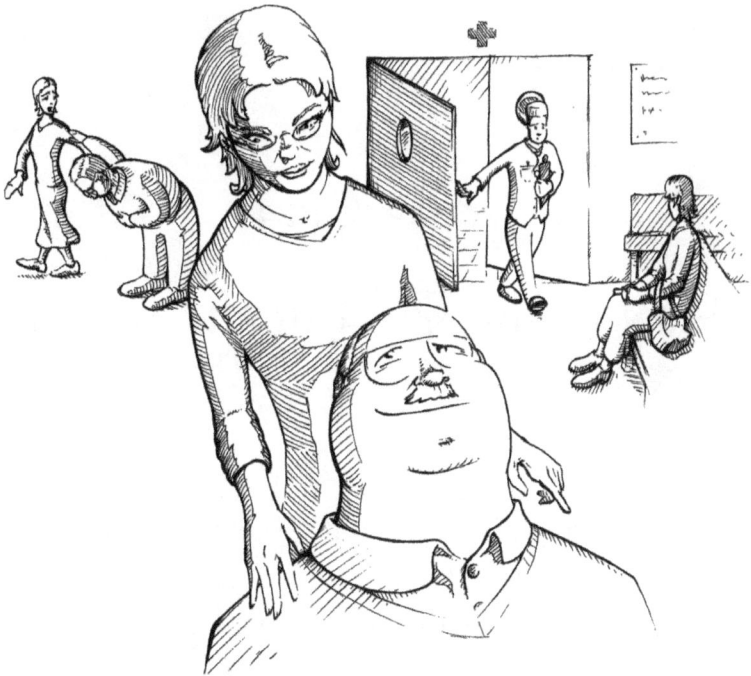

There is nothing magic about any of these techniques and beliefs, but they are difficult for sufferers to construct when consumed by their own black dog.

CHAPTER 24

Joy at the End of the Road

My great hope in this final chapter is that you, the reader, share with me the unconditional message of joy and fulfillment in your own lives when you become free from anxiety and depression.

My story hit a cross roads in chapter ten; after the experience with the Angel in the water tank my experience of the black dog has been largely free from fear or dread.

Certainly the condition of anxiety and depression has not completely disappeared; rather I have been blessed with a gradual healing process involving all the components and skill sets described in earlier chapters.

It really doesn't matter if we see the experience in the "water tank" as a real messenger from God; or if it was my mind taking control of the situation.

Whatever the source of the power, it was saying to me, *John, you will not succumb to this monster; you are needed in this world and you will prevail.*

I have a strong faith that the former is the case; that Christ's Angel was with me, not just on that terrible day, but through my whole life.

The result of this evolution is that abundant joy has returned to my life. I am confident that the black dog is locked up somewhere in my psyche and is no longer finding its way toward being a negative influence in my life.

I have also been more acutely sensitive to a spiritual force at work in my world, helping me regain my physical and mental health. I believe this spiritual force is always available to us; we just need to open our hearts and accept the invitation.

It seems that human beings always attempt to put labels on the mysteries of the world; thus we apply our personal labels to this spiritual entity. In Buddhism, I am told, the term is "Mindfulness"; in Islam "Ruh Al-Qudus". In Judaism the Spirit is known as "Ruach ha Qodesh", Hinduism, "Sheva", and in Christianity many terms are used but is principally known as "the Holy Ghost" or "the Holy Spirit".

Most, if not all of the world's major religions give credence to a spiritual force at work in our world that is available to all of us.

I believe it is the power of the Holy Spirit that ultimately has allowed me to develop the resilience necessary to minimize the negative effects of the black dog from my life, and thus from the lives of my loved ones.

I have not achieved total victory over the dog, and I know that I am vulnerable when my defenses are not all in place. This means that I need to be forever vigilant for the reappearance of the dog's grotesque face.

Nonetheless, there have been instances of late when, historically, the dog would relish the situation and cause me grief. But the dog has not appeared; rather I have had a feeling of well-being, of Grace and most of all a sense of the return of unqualified joy into my life.

I have developed a particular sensitivity to those people who have difficulty in listening to other people's stories, particularly when it involves vulnerability. Thus the challenge continues; I have to be brave and offer my experience to help individuals, society in all its branches and even the church, but I have to understand the need for us all to be sensitive to how our own behavior affects others and to help and care for each other...

I believe there is good reason for all readers who have travelled with me through this book, and who, themselves, struggle with their own anxiety and depression, to be encouraged by my story.

No matter how difficult life can become struggling with our black dogs, there is always the power of hope; but as I have attempted to describe, there is much, much more involved.

But I believe most of all, we have to be willing to allow the Holy Spirit to enter our hearts, God will certainly replace the adversary and give us grace.

We started on the journey through this book, with a poem, *Invictus*, by William Ernest Henley. We would like to conclude with some equally inspiring words courtesy of the theologian Paul Tillich from *The Shaking of the Foundations*:

> We cannot transform our lives, unless we allow them to be transformed by that stroke of grace. It happens; or it does not happen. And certainly it does not happen if we force it on ourselves, just as it shall not happen as long as we think, in our self-complacency, that we have no need of it.

> Grace strikes us when we are in great pain and restlessness. It strikes us when we walk through

the dark valley of meaningless and empty life. It strikes us when our disgust for our own being, our indifference, our weakness, our hostility, and our lack of direction and composure become intolerable to us.

It strikes us when, year after year, the longed-for perfection of life does not appear, when the old compulsions reign within us as they have for decades, when despair destroys all joy and courage.

Sometimes at that moment a wave of light breaks into our darkness, and it is as if a voice is saying:"You are accepted. You are accepted by that which is greater than you, and the name of which you do not know.

Do not ask for the name now; perhaps you will do much. Do not seek for anything; do not perform anything; do not intend anything. Simply accept the fact that you are accepted. If that happens to us, we experience grace.

EPILOGUE

The author believes that the very writing of this life story is a weapon in itself against the Black Dog. To understand anxiety and depression, to understand that it is a part of one's very persona, is to begin to remove the mystery.

The author has mildly adapted quotes from two authors on the subject of anxiety and depression that he believes underscore or complement much of what he has tried to convey to the reader of *The Black Dog*.

From John Sanford's *Healing and Wholeness* (1977):

> There is a force within us that always works to bring things into the light..., We do not "decide" to become whole; rather it is thrust upon us by the same life force within us.

The author would like to add that the life force within us is undoubtedly the power of the Holy Spirit at work in the world.

Sanford continues:

Mental distress is an illness on the same footing as any other; there is no reason to be ashamed if one suffers from anxiety, depression, or other psychological maladies.

Again from Sanford,

Until one is willing to face one's shadow, the dark side of one's life, the unconscious simply does not open up, and the forces of healing are locked within.

To adapt from C. J. Jung,

We should not just disregard the depression but rather we can learn so much for our recovery. What the neurotic may fling away as entirely worthless, contains the true gold we would never have found elsewhere.

This book has been written to help fellow sufferers who are at various stages down the road from darkness into sunlight. Most of all the author hopes that the reader will appreciate the power of the Holy Spirit in the process toward a healthy and vital life.

As described in the book, John's friend and associate, Alan Miller, has his own story to tell. It is a different kind of story but it still concerns his personal battle with his Black Dog.

Alan is a younger man and has further to travel on his road.

Please keep watch for Alan's own book hopefully to be published in the future. An undetermined title as of yet, but for John, sentimentally, it will always be "The Black Dog – The Next Generation".

God Bless all the readers of this book. John truly hopes that it helps to lighten your load in life and help you vanquish your own black dog .

ABOUT THE AUTHOR AND THE ILLUSTRATOR

Reverend John Richard Dolan

John was raised in Cardiff, Wales and has lived and worked in the United States for more than forty years. John is a British Chartered Accountant (CPA) and is an ordained Deacon in the Episcopal Church USA.

The Black Dog is a story of personal struggle and ultimate triumph. This victory is a result of hard work, but it could only be achieved with God's help, and the total commitment of his family.

John and his wife Karen, have two grown, married children Michelle and David, and three grandchildren.

Paul Joshua Egel

The Illustrator of *The Black Dog*, Paul Egel, is a Chicago native and a professional artist/illustrator. Paul received his BFA from Long Beach State University, California. Other places of study include Griffith University in Brisbane, Australia, and College of Du Page, Glen Ellyn, IL. More of his work can be viewed at: www.egelart.com

162

www.ingramcontent.com/pod-product-compliance
Lightning Source LLC
LaVergne TN
LVHW091258080426
835510LV00007B/317